WRITE AND SELL
YOUR FREE-LANCE ARTICLE

Write and Sell Your Free-Lance Article

A complete guide to the general and specialized article marketplace, with step-by-step instructions on how to write and sell magazine and newspaper articles

Linda Buchanan Allen

Publishers   THE WRITER, INC.   Boston

Copyright © 1991
by Linda Buchanan Allen

Excerpts from "Thanksgiving in Kathmandu," "Searching for a Dream House," "From River to Sea—in a Kayak," and "Discovering Plum Island—Off Season," all by Linda Buchanan Allen, are reprinted by permission of the author and *Merrimack Valley Sunday.*

"Nothing Like Going for the Gold," by Linda Buchanan Allen, originally appeared in *The Boston Globe,* November 6, 1988. Reprinted by permission of the author.

Excerpts from "How You Can Tell if It's Really Love?" and "Love Stories 1991" by Lyn LeGendre, originally appeared in *North Shore Magazine,* February 14, 1991. Reprinted by permission of the author.

Excerpt from "Single Parents," by Lyn LeGendre, originally appeared in *North Shore Magazine,* September 13, 1990. Reprinted by permission of the author.

Excerpt from "Best Bets for Bad Times," by Jeffrey Zygmont, originally appeared in *Boston Magazine,* August 1990.

Excerpt from "Is a Sunspace for You?," by Mary Flanagan, originally appeared in *The Family Handyman,* July/August 1990.

Library of Congress Cataloging in Publication Data

Allen, Linda Buchanan, 1955–
  Write and sell your free-lance article / by Linda Buchanan Allen.
    p. cm.
  ISBN 0-87116-164-8
  1. Authorship. 2. Authorship—Marketing. 3. Feature writing.
I. Title.
PN151.A47 1991
808'.02—dc20   91-27068
                                                              CIP

Printed in the United States of America

To Donald M. Murray
for tending my words

and to Minnie Mae Murray
for tending my garden

Contents

Introduction THE PROFESSIONAL WRITER   3

PART 1—TECHNIQUES
1. GATHERING AND FOCUSING IDEAS   11
2. THE QUERY   16
3. INTERVIEWS AND RESEARCH   29
4. DRAFTING YOUR ARTICLE   41
5. REVISING AND EDITING   49

PART 2—ARTICLE TYPES
6. PERSONAL EXPERIENCE   59
7. ROUND-UPS   65
8. HOW-TO OR SERVICE ARTICLES   69
9. PROFILES   74
10. FEATURE ARTICLES   79

PART 3—SPECIAL FIELDS
11. DEVELOPING A SPECIALTY   84
12. TRAVEL AND RECREATION   91
13. SPORTS AND FITNESS   99
14. HEALTH   105
15. HOBBIES, CRAFTS, AND COLLECTIBLES   111
16. HOME AND GARDEN   120
17. MONEY MATTERS   126
18. SCIENCE AND NATURE   134

PART 4—SELLING YOUR ARTICLE
19. FINDING MARKETS   138
20. THE BUSINESS SIDE—DOLLARS AND SENSE   146
21. COPING WITH FAILURE—AND SUCCESS   152

Acknowledgments

I would like to thank the following people for their contributions to and support of this book:

Sylvia K. Burack, publisher, The Writer, Inc., for her years of dedication to writers; and for her patience and guidance, gently leading me on when I thought I couldn't see;

Donald M. Murray, for his development of the query format and his comments on revision, and for his friendship;

David Goodman, for his sample query letter and comments on outdoor writing;

Lyn LeGendre, for the use of her articles on romance and single parenting, and for her comments on profile writing;

The following writers and editors, for their insights on the world of free-lance writing: Catherine Buni, Richard L. Elia, Marjorie Flathers, Helen Gifford, Joe Hebert, Tom McFarland, Susan Schauppner, William G. Scheller, and Dawn E. Reno;

Melanie L. Babendreier, fellow writer whose friendship I cannot do without;

And my husband Boyd, whose unyielding inner strength allows me to be the star, even when I don't deserve it.

Write and Sell Your Free-Lance Article

Introduction
The Professional Writer

You stare at the stark, white page. There are no words on it yet. You want to make the page yours, with sharp ideas, precise arguments, nouns and verbs that sing. You fidget, adjusting the spacing and margins on your typewriter. Outside, a dump truck rumbles by; the windows of your house shudder a little. A distant siren whines. Downstairs, someone flicks on the television; voices balloon into the room. You hear the hiss of a hot frying pan doused under the cold water faucet. Your alarm clock ticks slowly, like one pin after another dropping on your desk. With every moment, the tension grows tighter. You grow bored, and finally restless. You turn off your typewriter and get up from your desk. The empty page has won.

Relax. This happens to every writer. Even the most experienced writer faces the blank page and walks away from it in frustration and despair. But while the professional writer understands how to work through this frustration, how to identify and focus ideas, how to use writing time effectively, how to write for an audience, and how to work with editors, the nonprofessional has not yet learned how to overcome frustration and move on to write marketable material. The difference between the professional and the amateur has nothing to do with being paid; it has to do with attitude and work habits.

This book aims to teach you how to be a professional free-lance article writer, whether you plan to write one or two articles per year or hope to make free-lance article writing your full-time career. You'll learn how to gather ideas and identify markets; write queries; research, draft, and revise your articles; and begin writing in a variety of specialties. You'll also learn how to cope with rejection slips and reactions—positive and negative—to your published writing. All of these topics revolve around the blank page and the unique words that you as a writer place on it.

Developing Professional Work Habits

Forget the myth that "real" writers are suffering, starving individuals who write only when they are inspired. These people, if they did exist, could hardly get anything done. They couldn't pay their bills, and they'd hardly ever meet writing deadlines. Editors don't want to work with them because they aren't reliable; in short, they aren't professional. Most successful writers are just like you. But they treat writing as a job, whether it's part time or full time. They enjoy the creative aspect of writing—the discovery of a new image, the surprise of a chilling or apt phrase—but they tackle the work of writing just as they would any other job.

Professional work habits show that you take your writing seriously and help you get the job done, whether it's a 700-word column for your local newspaper or a fully researched, feature-length article for a national magazine. Whether you are a full-time or a part-time free-lance writer, you should develop professional work habits right at the beginning of your writing career. There is no one "right" way to work, as long as you are consistent in your habits. You'll need to modify them from time to time, even from project to project. But if you stick to a few basic rules that you have established for yourself, you'll find that you accomplish much more than you would if you approached writing haphazardly, as a hobby.

When do you write?

One successful writer I know follows the rule, "Never a day without a line." He never lets a day pass without writing something. He carries a notebook filled with fragments of ideas, events, occurrences, and experiences. But he takes this further: Each day he works on at least one of the several writing projects he has going at once—a textbook, novel, newspaper column, or poem. When the writing doesn't flow freely, he uses his own techniques to push it forward—or he switches to another project.

If you are just starting out, you probably aren't making your living by writing full time. You have a job outside the home, your own business, a family to care for, or all three. As a part-time writer, how do you make time to write? Like the full-time writer, you need to establish a schedule. Perhaps you'll get up an hour earlier than usual to write before breakfast, or you may prefer to write for a half hour every night after dinner. Or it might mean that you write for an hour or two each Saturday and Sunday morning. If you have a full-time outside job, you can write during your lunch hours. (By doing that, you'll add a full five hours each week to your writing time.) Don't depend on a single, week-long vacation to write. If you haven't established a writing schedule year round that fits your regular work week, you won't accomplish much on the vacation because writing won't be part of your daily routine.

If you set up a writing routine and stick to it, you will begin to view your writing as an important job, and your family and friends will take their cues from you. You'll have some conflicts, and you'll have to reinforce your schedule periodically, but when your articles appear in print, family and friends will begin to respect and even defend your rules. Remember, every job—including writing—has some type of regular schedule.

Where do you write?

Having an established writing place helps you structure your writing routine. Most of us don't have the luxury of an isolated log cabin or a private study lined with walnut bookcases. Some writers are lucky enough to have a whole room to themselves; others stake out a corner of a room or even the kitchen table. But every writer needs a regular place where there is a minimum of distractions and where notes, manuscripts, reference books, and writing tools can be stored. It takes flexibility and sometimes a struggle to set up the writing place and writing routine; but all professional writers have found a way to balance their writing jobs with the demands made on the other segments of their lives.

Tools of the trade

Just as writers have different ways of working, they also prefer different tools of the trade. Some prefer to write rough drafts longhand, then transfer what they've written to the typewriter. Others compose directly on typewriters or word processors. Many use a combination of tools, depending on the needs of each project.

There is no question that word processors have changed writers' lives in many ways. Composing is often quicker. Revising—playing with words, moving paragraphs, rewriting entire sections—is easier with a word processor than it is with a typewriter. In addition, a writer can offer an editor both hard copy (manuscript) and a computer disk if the publication's word-processing program is compatible with the writer's. But remember: A word processor won't make you a better or more successful writer, and there is no reason to run out and buy one at the beginning of your writing career. Many professional writers still use typewriters, or even write by hand.

If you choose to use a typewriter as your main writing tool, keep it clean and in good working order, so your manuscripts have no smudges or filled-in letters, and thus are easy for the editor to read.

If you prefer to compose your first draft in longhand, fine. Just make sure that you can read your own handwriting so it can be easily transcribed later, because you *must* submit manuscripts, queries, and correspondence to an editor in typewritten form, either from a typewriter or from a word processor.

Keep a good supply of your other tools on hand—ribbons, correction tape, typing paper, legal-size pads for writing longhand, pens, pencils, erasers, paper clips, rubber bands, 8½" × 11" envelopes, stationery, and so forth—so that you don't run out in the middle of an article.

Once you've published several articles, consider ordering simple business stationery and business cards. These don't have to be elaborate; they should include your professional name (the name you use when writing), address, and phone number. You can order them through almost any office-supply store or even department store. (Do not have a line reading "Professional Writer" or the equivalent.)

Working with Editors

Throughout your writing career, you will work with many different types of editors. Editors are human beings. They have good days and bad days, just as you do. A few guidelines can help you develop good relationships with editors.

Unless absolutely necessary, write, do not telephone, an editor—especially for your initial contact. A phone call out of the blue interrupts a busy editor and puts him or her on the spot; a well-written letter allows the editor a chance to think about what you've said or asked before responding.

Maintain a friendly, professional attitude with an editor; don't pour out your feelings about your struggles as a writer or your love for the written word. When talking with an editor, keep the conversation focused on the article you are writing, and avoid discussing personal matters.

Learn to be a good listener. Ask the editor as many questions as you need to, and listen to the answers. Take notes during your conversation; repeat them to the editor to confirm any points you are not entirely certain about. If you have previously written to the editor to inquire about an article idea and are now discussing this on the phone, note carefully the type and focus of the piece the editors wants—not the article you think you'd like to write.

If you are already working on an article and have questions about it, call or write to the editor with specific and concrete questions; then be attentive to the editor's responses. If the discussion has dealt with major issues, summarize the decisions you've agreed on in a follow-up letter to the editor.

Keep your editor apprised of the progress of an article, especially if it is one that will take more than a week or so to complete. This is especially important if you get into a piece and realize that it's not going to work; call or write the editor and explain your difficulties. By discussing things, you and the editor might be able to work out an alternate approach for the article. If not, at least you won't have lost a lot of your time and the editor's working on an article that is unlikely to be published. And the editor will remember—and appreciate—your frankness and professionalism.

If you have listened well, you know what the editor has asked for; that's the article that he or she is counting on for publication. If, for example, you have agreed to write an article on how homeowners can have their drinking water tested for impurities, don't write about the benefits of buying bottled water. The editor will be annoyed that you ignored his or her guidelines, and will be wary of encouraging you to write another article. And, worst of all, the article you did write won't appear in that publication.

Meet your deadlines. If the editor is counting on your article for a particular issue of the magazine or newspaper, be sure you get it there on time. If you miss a deadline, the editor may have to scramble to find another article to fill the space that was allocated for your piece. And if your article was slated to be the main feature of the magazine or newspaper issue, with relevant ads, the advertising manager will have to notify advertisers, who must then decide whether to keep their ads in the current issue or postpone them to a later issue. If while you are working on your article you find that you are uncovering a larger story than you and the editor had realized, or if you are absolutely sure you can't meet the deadline, phone the editor immediately so that you and the editor can work out an alternate date. It is the editor's choice, not yours, whether to delay publication of your article or to accept a shorter piece to appear when originally scheduled.

Learn to accept editing. No one's writing is infallible, and it is your job to provide editors with articles that they want to offer their readers. An editor is trained to read manuscripts for content, organization, and clarity, keeping the publication's readers in mind. You are free to question the editor, or to discuss points of editing that you don't agree with, but a truly professional writer is able to accept change and suggestions that frequently result in a better article.

Begin forming your professional attitude and developing good work habits before you complete your first article, and you've taken your first steps toward becoming a successful professional free-lance writer.

Techniques

1

Gathering and Focusing Ideas

You already know that you want to write an article. But what do you want to write about? Writers know that ideas come from all aspects of life. A person who reads, keeps up with the news, engages in discussions with others, listens well, and has particular interests—whether they are in business, foreign places, health and fitness, hobbies, or scientific discoveries—has something to write about. The key is to identify that something.

What to write about: sources

Ideas may come to you while you're driving to work, mowing the lawn, or shopping for groceries. Learn to see your world and experiences in it as discrete parts of the larger story of human experience. Different aspects of life, and the unique ways they connect, make good ideas for articles. Often several events fuse to make a single idea for an article. For example, conversations with several female friends who are starting their own businesses from their homes might get your mind working on an idea about women entrepreneurs. Or running in several road races might lead to an idea about competitive runners over age fifty.

There is no single good idea for an article. Nor is there any one "right" way to gather ideas for articles; but here are several approaches you can try:

1. *Be observant.* Increase your awareness of the world around you. Pay attention to the details of conversations, events, and experiences in which you are engaged. Observe how you and others react to different situations. Use all of the five senses: Recall the color of a person's sweater, especially if it's unusual; the sound of a car door slamming; the texture of new snow; the scent and taste of fresh coffee.

2. *Read.* Be an avid reader. Read books, magazines, and newspapers, and even advertisements and junk mail for ideas. A headline in a newspaper or a quote in a magazine article may be enough to spark an idea. Reading magazines and newspapers not only keeps you abreast of current events, but also familiarizes you with particular publications.

3. *Collect information.* Keep a notebook, and jot down facts, observations, reactions, and thoughts you can use later as your idea bank.

4. *Draw on your own knowledge.* Think about what you already know. Your job, hobbies, and other special interests can be fodder for articles. If you work in the insurance field, for example, you might decide to write an article on how car owners can choose the best auto insurance. If you are an avid cook, you might offer readers tips for quick kitchen clean-up. If you're particularly knowl-

edgeable about a major historical event, such as the Civil War, you might want to write about a group that reenacts the battles of the Civil War.

5. *Use your imagination.* Consider an unfamiliar topic that you'd like to know more about. Don't avoid a subject just because you're not an expert on it. Good research will help you become informed enough to write an authoritative piece.

6. *Use your memory.* Connect your own experiences with present events. Once, while I was at a college hockey game, I began to remember all the games of pond hockey my brothers and I had played when we were children. These thoughts led to an idea for a piece on the difference between formal, organized sports and informal games, such as between "backyard" croquet and American Croquet Club rules.

Focusing Ideas

Once you have selected a general topic, you need to focus it. For example, if your general idea is viewing fall foliage in New England, which is much too broad for one article, you might narrow the topic to seeing the foliage from a canoe. Three factors help you focus your idea: market, audience, and type of article. (See Part Two for discussion of article types.)

Markets

Your market is the magazine or newspaper to which you plan to present your idea. Each magazine and newspaper has characteristics that distinguish it from other publications. It's up to you as a free-lance writer to read thoroughly several issues of any magazine or newspaper you intend to write for (including the articles, the letters to the editor, the ads, and the editorial page) before presenting your idea to the editor. As you study a publication, begin to focus your idea so that it fits the general characteristics of the magazine. Nothing marks the nonprofessional more quickly than the article idea that is clearly inappropriate for the publication. If you do your homework, you'll save yourself time and aggravation; and chances are, you'll find an editor who likes your idea much more quickly. (See Chapter 19 for more on markets.)

Audience

Every publication has an audience: its readers. As you study its contents, think about the readers. What are they interested in? What do they need to know and want to know about a topic? Are they experts in a field or general readers? Do they live in a particular region or are they scattered across the country? Above all, readers care about a subject as it relates to *them*. For example, if you plan to write about viewing fall foliage from a canoe for a regional magazine in New England, your readers are apt to live in New England but aren't expert canoeists. So they'll want to know where to rent canoes, where to find scenic rivers that have calm water for beginners, and even how to paddle a canoe. And they'll want to know what *different* views of the foliage one gets from canoeing on a river.

Trends

Keep up-to-date on trends. Subjects that were once of great interest to readers may no longer be current, and vice versa. Subjects that were once taboo, such as alcoholism, death, or child abuse, are now written about extensively in all kinds of publications. Watch for changes in public attitude; it wasn't long ago that environmentalists were considered part of the counterculture, and they certainly weren't accepted as scientists. Now environmentalism is big business.

2

THE QUERY

AN ARTICLE QUERY IS JUST WHAT it sounds like: a question. The query is your written approach to an editor, offering him or her your idea for an article. Your query should provide all the information the editor needs to decide whether or not your article idea is likely to appeal to the readers of that publication. If the editor likes your query, you may get the go-ahead to write a piece either on speculation or on assignment.

An assignment is a verbal or written contract between writer and editor for a particular article. "On speculation" means that, while the editor is interested in seeing your article, he or she is not willing or ready at this stage to make the firm offer for your piece. Some publications accept material only on speculation; others give assignments only to established writers. In either case, many writers work on speculation, and certainly beginning writers should expect to write only on speculation until they are well established.

QUERY VS. UNSOLICITED MANUSCRIPT

You think you have a great idea for an article and you know just the right publication for it. You're sure that the editor, given a chance to read your article, will buy it on the spot. Not necessarily. While some markets and editors do accept unsolicited manuscripts (say, personal experience articles), most prefer to receive a query first.

The query saves both you and the editor time and effort. It lets the editor think over your proposal; it provides a sample of your writing and gives the necessary background information about you. The editor doesn't have to wade through pages and pages of manuscript to decide whether the article will meet the publication's needs. An editor can always find a few minutes to read a good query, but might not get around to a completed manuscript for weeks. By then, you will be frustrated—and the story may be out of date. From the writer's point of view, a query will take only from one-half hour to a few hours to write; an entire article, complete with research, can take weeks. If the editor doesn't give you a go-ahead based on a query, you've lost only a few hours' work; if a complete manuscript is rejected, you've lost much more time and effort.

A query provides flexibility for the editor and the writer. If the editor likes the general idea but wants to change the focus, that can be agreed upon before the writer even begins to write the article. If, on the other hand, you submit a completed manuscript and the editor suggests a different approach, you will have to rewrite and restructure the whole manuscript.

Send your query directly to the editor (by name) of a particular department, or to the general editor (often called a managing editor or editor-in-chief) for feature articles. Don't address your query just to "Editor"; it will probably languish without ever reaching the right person. Check the masthead of the most recent issue of a publication (usually located near the beginning of the magazine) to find the right editor's name. Or call the office and ask.

Anatomy of a Magazine or Newspaper

Most magazines and newspapers have separate sections or departments that cover different topics or areas of interest. A single issue usually includes several long feature articles, then a number of shorter articles within special interest sections. The table of contents of many magazines identifies the features and several different departments, including such topics as business, health, travel, house and garden, parenting, fashion, arts and books, science, money matters, letters to the editor, and so forth.

See whether the bylines on various articles in the issue match the names of staff members on the masthead; this will give you an idea of what sections of the publication are staff-written and which accept free-lance material. If *all* of the articles are written by staff members, chances are the editor doesn't accept material from free lancers; if some appear to be written by free lancers, request writers' guidelines. If you have only one issue of the magazine, request a few back issues or look them up in your library. (Back issues are generally not free.) Both of these requests should precede your query, and both should include a self-addressed stamped envelope (SASE), or sufficient money for sample issues.

Study the entire publication carefully, then each of its departments to determine where your article idea would be most appropriate. Letters to the editor, the editorial page, and even the advertisements help you establish the magazine or newspaper's focus and the nature of the audience it reaches. The articles provide a sample of the style and range of subjects in which the editor is interested. You can also determine which topics have been recently covered.

Telephone or Typewriter?

Never telephone an editor before sending a *written* query. Editors of magazines and newspapers work under tight deadlines and often have an overwhelming amount of work. Of course, good editors are always on the lookout for new writers and story ideas—but they will appreciate the new writers who make their jobs a little easier. If you phone—even if the editor is available and seemingly interested in you and your idea—chances are you'll be asked to submit a written query anyway.

So head for your typewriter. It is, after all, the medium through which you plan to communicate with readers. A written query gives the editor the opportunity to read and reread your idea, mull it over, discuss it with colleagues. Instead of the flat "no" that you may get from a telephone query because of distractions or lack of time, you might just get a "yes" from your written query. Or the editor might decide that although the specific idea you have proposed isn't appropriate for the publication, he or she likes your writing well enough to discuss another article idea with you.

Ten Elements of a Query

Although a good query anticipates and answers the questions an editor may have about your article idea and provides him or her with enough information to decide whether or not to give you the go-ahead to write the article, it obviously cannot convey everything you know about your topic. The article itself does that. The query should, however, cover the following ten points:

1. *Your name, address, and phone number.* Make it easy for the editor to get in touch with you. If you plan to be out of town for a week or more, mention this, including times and dates you will be available by phone. If you plan to use a pen name for your byline on the article, make this clear, and state the reason.

2. *General topic and focused idea.* Your general topic might be outdoor decks attached to houses; your focused idea might be how homeowners can build their own 12' by 12' deck. Your focused idea should also include your main point. For example, do you plan to emphasize the ease with which a deck can be built or its low cost?

3. *Purpose and type of article.* Is your purpose to recount a personal experience, or to explain where or how to do something, to round up information on a topic, to present a profile of a celebrity, or to develop a topic in depth? Your purpose indicates what type of article you are planning to write, and should be included in your query.

4. *Point of view.* Your query should indicate that you feel strongly about a topic and have a definite point of view. You aren't *looking* for an idea—you are *presenting* one. This doesn't mean that the point of view should be exaggerated or sentimental, but simply that you have a story to tell and a point to make. For example, if you plan to write an article about a food market cooperative, your point of view might be that consumers can save money by shopping this way.

5. *Length.* Reading several issues of the publication will tell you the length of average articles in it. Market lists in writers' magazines also include desired wordage

along with other editorial requirements. Don't propose a 3,000-word article if the maximum article length is 1,500 words. By the same token, make sure the length is appropriate to cover your story idea.

6. *Major points that the article will cover.* Include the four or five most important points you will make in your article. If the article explains a process, the major points would describe the main steps in the process.

7. *Tone.* Your query will show the editor whether the tone will be personal, humorous, or formal. Write your introductory paragraph (see Query Format) in the tone you plan to use in the article itself.

8. *How you plan to research your article.* State whether you know experts in the field, if you plan to travel to obtain information, or if you have personal experience with the topic. If your topic is seasonal—say, involving blossoming times of famous gardens or the migration of birds—mention when and where you plan to conduct your research. If you plan to take 35-mm photos as part of your research, offer color slides or black-and-white glossy prints; but in many cases the publication prefers to provide its own.

9. *Your qualifications as a writer on the subject of your proposed article.* Of course, you should mention any recently published articles that are relevant to your subject (letters to the editor of a newspaper don't count). If you are a new writer, or a writer branching into a new field, list articles you have published in other fields, if any, or relevant work experience. For example, if you plan to write an article on the success of small businesses started by women in your region, it will help if the editor knows that you are a business consultant with an M.B.A. who has worked with these women.

10. *Sidebar.* Sometimes a query has a tenth element: a proposed sidebar. A sidebar is the separate box in a newspaper or magazine article that offers tips or facts that do not appear in the body of the article. It might be a checklist of necessary steps in preparing to paint a house, a list of country inns with names, addresses, and rates, best ways to travel, important sites in the area, or tips for bicycling safely. Even if you don't propose a sidebar in your query, the editor may suggest one to you.

Query Format

Although many writers successfully use letters for queries, the letter form has some drawbacks. First, a letter may contain information that isn't relevant to the query itself—for example, your introduction of yourself to the editor. If the editor decides to pass your query along to the head of a specific department at the magazine or newspaper, that person would then have to read the irrelevant information in order to get to the query itself. Second, it can be hard for the editor to distinguish between the writing style you use in your letter and the writing style and tone you plan to use in your article. So I use an alternative, an adaptation of a format developed by a colleague of mine who has been a published writer for fifty years.

This format includes a proposed title for the article, which although it may change, gives the editor a feeling for the "theme" and direction of the article. It includes a sample opening paragraph, which establishes the writer's style and covers the main points of the article with a bulleted list. This format also makes it possible for the editor to remove my separate cover letter, photocopy the query, and pass it to other editors of the publication who may be involved in the decision making. I wrote the following query in this format, for *The Boston Globe*.

Linda Buchanan Allen
Address
Phone number

HITTING THE TRAIL FOR DAY HIKES

Day hiking is exactly what it sounds like: hiking for a day. You leave your house on a bright morning and return in the evening, tired, a little dirty, and happy. You sleep in your own bed at night. No campgrounds. No tents. No RVs. You've spent your day tromping the trails of New England toward a mountain summit, kicking up a little dust, leaping a stream, munching your lunch on a sunny rock while enjoying the view.

****

As the weather grows warmer, *Globe* readers will be looking for outdoor adventures for themselves and their children—both on weekends and during summer vacation. "Hitting the Trail for Day Hikes," approximately 2,000 words, will offer readers specific itineraries for day hikes that are within a day's drive of Boston and that can be managed and enjoyed by both adults and school-age children. Day hikes are more challenging than local nature walks; each hike involves hiking a trail toward the summit of a hill or small mountain.

"Hitting the Trail for Day Hikes" will cover the following:
• *Where to Go.* Driving times, location of trail heads, hiking times/distances, and information on terrain will be provided for the following mountains. I have hiked all of the trails myself and have access to maps and trail descriptions.

For beginners, or children ages 6 and up: Blue Hills Reservation, Mt. Wachusett, Mt. Agamenticus (eastern Massachusetts and southern Maine)

For slightly more experienced hikers, or children ages 8 and up: Mt. Monadnock (western Massachusetts)

For hikers in good condition and children ages 10 and up: Mt. Osceola, Mt. Moosilauke, Mt. Chocorua (White Mountains of New Hampshire)

- *What to Take.* Includes the "ten essentials" every hiker needs, as well as recommended gear.
- *What to Wear.* Includes tips on layering for New England weather.
- *What to Eat.* Includes tips on easy, non-perishable, high-energy snacks for the trail.
- *Safety Tips.* Includes tips on blisters, drinking water, setting a "turnaround time," checking the weather, safe walking techniques, etc.

About the writer

My book, *High Mountain Challenge: A Guide for Young Mountaineers,* is due to be published by Appalachian Mountain Club Books in July 1989. I have written on travel and the outdoors for publications such as *The New York Times,* and had a column in the *Globe*'s "Living Forum" last November. I lead trips and teach workshops for the Appalachian Mountain Club, including beginner backpacking, family backpacking, and backcountry skiing. I have hiked and climbed mountains in the United States, Switzerland, and Nepal.

Note that the query covered nine points listed in Elements of a Query. (Although I didn't propose a sidebar in my query, the editor created one from the tips I gave in the article on what to take, what to wear, and what to eat.) The editor gave me the go-ahead and the article was published a few months later.

Once you have written several articles for a publication and have come to know the editor, a query in letter format works just fine. The editor is already familiar with your background and writing skills. The following is an example of an informal query letter to an editor who already knows the writer. This writer specializes in health-care as well as other subjects; the publication is *American Medical News*.

Dear (name of editor):
Following is the query that I ran by you on the phone a few weeks ago.
Heart attacks—About 1.5 million Americans suffer heart attacks each year, one third of which are fatal. In recent years, new technology has been revolutionizing critical care for cardiac patients and promises to improve survival rates for heart attack victims dramatically. The recent introduction of defibrillators into basic ambulance units in a number of cities around the country, current experiments with implanted defibrillators, the wider use of "miracle" cardiac drugs such as TPA and streptokinase, combined with increasing awareness of CPR, have improved the chances of survival—in the short term. However, the improvement in emergency treatment has not necessarily translated into increased life expectancy for the average sedentary American.
This piece would look briefly at the latest advancements in emergency cardiac care, and focus on the controversy that these developments have spawned. Are dollars and priorities well placed when we are giving expensive temporary reprieves to patients who are statistically at great risk of suffering a fatal heart attack in the near future? What do cardiologists think of the trend toward decentralizing invasive emergency cardiac procedures? Are low-level EMT's really qualified to do such work? What have been the results

in test locations (such as Boston) where these advanced emergency procedures are being attempted in the field? I would examine the ethical, economic and medical controversies that have evolved as we get better at bringing heart attack victims back from the brink.

Please drop me a note or give me a call and let me know your thoughts on this story idea.

                        Sincerely,
                        (Name of writer)

This query answers the questions that the editor might have. The writer presents the issue—or controversy—and the main points that the article will cover. He tells the editor what his approach will be, and where (test locations) he plans to obtain some of his information. He uses a writing style that is appropriate to the article itself: informative but gripping. And he shows the editor that he is knowledgeable about his subject by using correct terminology *(defibrillators, CPR).*

Whichever format you choose, keep the following tips for query writing in mind:

Timing. Magazines work at least six months and sometimes a year ahead of the publication date. Thus, if you want to propose an article on great summer walking tours, plan to send your query to the magazine editor during the winter or fall *before* the article would be published (up to one year ahead). If your article idea requires you to take certain walking tours for research, submit your query even earlier—in the spring—to give the editor time to make a decision and give you the go-ahead. Allow about six weeks for the editor to review a query before you follow up with a letter or phone call.

Newspapers work more quickly than magazines—from

a few weeks to a few months ahead of the publication date, depending on the type of piece that's involved. If you want to write a seasonal piece like the one on summer walking tours, send your query to the newspaper editor during the spring immediately preceding the summer you want to see the article published. If you plan to write an article on a subject that is timely—say, the shutting down of a manufacturing plant in your area on a certain date—don't wait. Try to anticipate the event and submit your query well ahead of time. Then be prepared to write the article under a tight deadline. Give a newspaper editor two to three weeks to review a query.

Payment. Your query should *not* discuss payment. That comes later, after the editor gives you the go-ahead to write the article.

Cover letter. If you are using the first format for your query, include a cover letter that introduces you to the editor and states your idea and the focus of the proposed article in a sentence or two. Also indicate when you could have the article ready, and offer to provide any clips you may have of your previously published articles, if the editor would like to see a sample of your published writing. Your cover letter should be in regular business format, on good paper.

Proofread. This is your only chance to make a first impression on the editor as a professional writer. Nothing turns an editor off more quickly than a letter or query that is filled with typos or grammatical errors. Be sure that you have spelled the editor's name correctly. One magazine editor who has an unusual name refuses to read queries that do not spell her name correctly; if they don't, she knows at once the writers have not paid attention to detail and accuracy.

Mail. Mail your query and letter in a 10″ × 13″ envelope first class, making sure you have attached enough postage (so that the query doesn't arrive with postage due). There's no need to use certified or registered mail.

Take time in writing your query. The quality of your query can make the difference between rejection and acceptance. A complete, well-crafted query is the mark of a professional and is often the start of a good relationship between writer and editor.

3

INTERVIEWS AND RESEARCH

An editor has given you the go-ahead to write an article you've proposed in a query. If you are new to article writing, most likely it will be on speculation. Now what? Chances are, you aren't ready to write your article yet. Many articles require at least some research. There are a number of ways to do this.

Interviews

Just about every article involves people. Even if your piece doesn't center on a particular person (as in a profile), it's likely that you'll need to talk to or correspond with some knowledgeable person or expert on your subject for information or verification of some points. Interviews, therefore, are important tools for the writer. There are three types of interviews: in-person, telephone, and mail.

The in-person interview

The in-person interview provides you with the most data, in depth and breadth. When you feel that you need to consult an expert for information or authoritative opinions that you can use in your article, you may feel a bit nervous or apprehensive about conducting the required interview. It's a little like stage fright: It keeps you on your toes. But don't worry. Even if you don't entirely overcome your initial shyness, you'll learn to cope with it as part of being a free-lance writer. And in most instances, after a friendly conversation with your subject, you'll wonder why you were nervous in the first place.

Where do you start? First, make sure you have the correct spelling and pronunciation of the person's name and his or her correct address and/or telephone number. Then write to the person to request an interview, identifying yourself, providing the name of the magazine or newspaper you are writing for (if you have a go-ahead or an assignment), and briefly state what your article is about. Explain that you are doing research for the article and ask for an appointment to discuss a particular aspect of the piece. (Of course, if you wish to write a profile, explain that.) Ask for a specific amount of time—say, half an hour or an hour (unless you are writing an in-depth profile, in which case you would want a longer interview).

If the interviewee calls or writes agreeing to an interview, set a date, time, and place that are acceptable to both of you, but be as flexible as you can, deferring to your interviewee's schedule whenever possible. When you've settled these details, write a note thanking him or her, confirming the appointment.

An interview is most often conducted in the person's workplace, home, or even a nearby restaurant. (If you choose a restaurant, make sure it is a relatively quiet one—and be prepared to pick up the check; the interviewee is your guest. But don't expect the publication to reimburse you unless you have arranged that with the editor in advance.) Sometimes you'll find yourself in unusual surroundings. The interview I had the most fun on recently took place in a Jeep, when I toured a wildlife refuge with the assistant refuge manager. I had a hard time scribbling notes as we jounced along, but I saw every inch of the refuge and caught firsthand her enthusiasm for her job, all of which was reflected in the article that I eventually wrote and sold.

Next, go back to your query and think through what information you want to gain from this interview. Based on what you already know, frame questions that will fill in the gaps. Make a list of the questions, both general and specific, that you plan to ask. This will help you focus on the information and facts you need and will keep the conversation from straying too far off the mark. A good basis for framing questions is the standard journalistic formula: Who? What? When? Where? How? Why? For example, if you are writing an article on a woman whose drunk driving accident caused her to become an advocate for MADD (Mothers Against Drunk Driving), you might ask, "Who was involved in the accident?" "What actually happened on the morning of the trial?" "When did you realize that there was another person involved?" "Where were you when you heard the news?" "How did you overcome your difficulties?" "Why did you choose that course of action?"

Such preparation will indicate that you are serious about your task and that you don't expect the interviewee to do your work for you. During the interview, you don't have to follow your questions in order, nor should you interrupt a valuable digression in the conversation to ask your next question. But you'll be armed with ideas and some general direction for the conversation.

Be sure that you have a fresh notepad and several pens for note-taking. If you plan to use a tape recorder, check to see that it's in good working order; carry an extra battery and blank tape in case you need it.

Before beginning an interview in which you plan to use a tape recorder, you must ask permission of the interviewee to do so; then record the interviewee granting permission. Before taking notes, ask the person to sign a simple release form giving you permission to use in the article the information he or she provides in the interview. It's always best to use the name of the person you are quoting in your article; however, if your subject insists on anonymity, your release form should reflect that agreement.

Remember that your interview subject may be as nervous as you are. Since the focus of the discussion is going to be on him or her, you'll go a long way toward relieving your own anxiety by trying to make your interviewee feel comfortable. Most people talk freely once they are relaxed. When you meet, spend a few minutes chatting—about mutual interests, your surroundings, even people whom you both know—to establish an informal atmosphere and guide the conversation into the interview from there.

Begin the actual interview with a specific question that the interviewee can later develop or expand upon (but don't attack your subject with your toughest question first). Try to weave your next questions into the fabric of the conversation as if you were chatting with a friend over a cup of coffee. For example, I began by asking the assistant manager of the wildlife refuge how many rare piping plovers were nesting on the beach. Then I asked her why it was important for visitors to avoid walking near the plovers' nests. Finally, I asked her about her views on the protection of endangered and threatened species.

Look at the speaker while he or she is talking and listen carefully. Make some comment or response so that the speaker knows you are attentive. Don't allow yourself to be distracted. Be encouraging, not judgmental. If the person says something that offends you, don't launch into a tirade or express *your* outrage. Just ask, "Why do you feel that way?" The answer might be a gem of insight. If the person seems to be groping for an answer, be patient. If he or she doesn't seem to be forthcoming about anything at all, try offering a bit of information about yourself to prompt the interviewee into talking. But be wary of taking over the conversation. "You always want to listen more than you talk," advises a writer who specializes in writing profiles. "And you want to get as many anecdotes as you can, something that speaks volumes about the person."

As you take notes, don't try to write down everything that the person says; you'll only be frustrated and disrupt the flow of conversation. Jot down key words and phrases. If the person says something that you want to quote, write that down; don't be afraid to ask the person to repeat or clarify the statement if necessary.

Be sure you keep within the agreed-upon time limit (without consulting your watch too frequently or obviously). When the interview is over, shake hands with your interviewee and thank him or her sincerely, even if the interview didn't go as well as you had hoped. And *always* follow up with a brief, friendly thank-you note. Graciousness is the sign of a true professional, and assures you a cordial response to any follow-up contact you need to make.

The telephone interview

Sometimes a telephone interview is necessary: You

might not be able to travel to see the person, or you just need to ask a few questions. Phone interviews are sometimes preferred by celebrities and by people whose time is limited or who frequently are approached or consulted as experts. Many of the guidelines for the in-person interview apply to the phone interview.

A telephone recording device, available at small cost, can be a great asset to the phone interview: It connects to your telephone and enables you to record the interview as conducted over the telephone. Stores that sell tape recorders or telephones are likely to have this device.

When you reach the person you wish to interview by phone, introduce yourself, state your purpose, and if he or she is agreeable, ask what would be the most convenient time for an interview, suggesting a specific length of time—twenty minutes, a half hour, or whatever you think such an interview would take to cover the questions you think you'll need to ask. Be prepared with your questions, your recording device, and your pad and pencil in case he surprises you and says, "I'll be away next week, but I have a few minutes right now." If you set the time of a phone interview for a later date, be sure to call at the exact time you agreed upon. If the person agrees to the interview when you make your first call, ask if you may send a simple release form for the subject to sign. This should clearly state that you have permission to use the information to be provided in the phone interview in your article.

In a phone interview, you'll probably spend less time chatting at the beginning than you would at an in-person interview. Listen carefully as you take down notes. Encourage your subject with appropriate interjections such as "of course," or "I understand." Dealing with lulls in phone conversations can be more difficult than with those in personal interviews, but you can cover these with related questions or those that evolve as the conversation progresses. You can also turn the questioning in an entirely different direction to get things moving again.

Keep your watch within sight so that you don't go over the time you agreed to. When you reach that moment, wait for a natural break in the conversation. If you have all the information you need, thank the interviewee and conclude the phone call on a friendly note, following up with a thank-you note. If you think you need more time, ask your subject whether you may continue or schedule another interview for a later date.

The mail interview

In some instances, an interview by mail is your only option. Although mail interviews don't allow you to adjust your questions to the personality or interests of your interviewee, and certainly cut down on spontaneity, they do give the interviewee a chance to think through answers thoroughly and reduce the danger of inadvertent misquoting.

Introduce yourself and state that you have a go-ahead from a magazine or newspaper to write an article on a subject in which the person is an acknowledged authority. Then ask if the person would be willing to answer a few questions to supply you with information you need and to verify certain information or facts relevant to the topic. If you wish to quote the interviewee directly, say so, but offer him or her the option of remaining anonymous except by title ("an eminent astronomer at a major university," or the "head of a prominent research institution," or "a doctor who was part of a team that made a breakthrough discovery in biogenetics"). It is important, however, to offer anonymity only as a last resort in gaining consent for an interview, since it would obviously weaken the impact and validity of the "testimony."

List your questions on a separate sheet of paper. Leave spaces after each question, or indicate that the person may prefer to write the answers or comments on separate sheets. Questions should be open-ended so that they will require more than a simple "yes" or "no" answer. Try to keep your questions to fewer than ten—but don't leave out an important question just to keep the number small. Make your questions clear, so that you will elicit just the information you want and need to write an authoritative article.

Close your letter by asking the person to sign an enclosed release form, and be sure to include a self-addressed, stamped envelope for the reply.

Allow two to three weeks for a response; if you don't hear anything, follow up with a short, friendly note. If you receive a response—whether the letter is detailed or brief—be sure to acknowledge it.

RESEARCH

Libraries

There is no better single source of information, inspiration, and ideas than libraries—public, academic, specialized (business libraries or those that you have access to in large corporations, insurance companies), state historical libraries, large and small. Even after you have settled on the topic for your article, but don't know where to start, go to the library to browse or to dig for information in books, microfilms and microfiche of scientific and unusual publications, or up-to-the-minute facts in their pamphlet files.

The reference librarian will help you locate many kinds of material on the subject you are researching and may help you narrow down the sources you need to consult. The card catalogue and indexes that relate to such special areas as education, science, industry, business, and medicine will not only help pinpoint just what you need, but will also lead you to the newest writing on the subject. These indexes are similar in set-up to the *Readers' Guide to Periodical Literature,* which indexes articles by subject, author, and title from a large number of periodicals. Many good public libraries subscribe to a large number of magazines, newspapers, and general as well as specialized publications. If the books and periodicals you are looking for are not available in your library, the librarian can often obtain them from other libraries through the interlibrary loan system, an extraordinarily useful resource.

Research by computer

If you have a computer equipped with a modem, it can provide you with a wealth of research material. A modem is a telecommunications device that allows your computer to access other computers by phone. Don't make the investment in a modem unless you plan to use it for more than just a few articles.

Shared computer information falls into two general categories: 1) networks, which tie several computers together to access mutual files; and 2) databases, which are collections of information that can be accessed by computer. Nonprofit organizations, universities, corporations, and computer societies sometimes have networks and/or databases available to the public either at no charge or for a small fee. To learn more about these, call the organization, university, corporation, or society and ask whether it has any relevant computer networks or databases available to the public for research.

Other resources

Many companies, nonprofit organizations, and government agencies are happy to provide you with statistics and other information you need for your article. Consult the phone book (both yellow and white pages) or library reference department for names and addresses, and contact the public relations director of the company, organization, or agency in the same way you would a person for an interview, identifying yourself, the magazine or newspaper for which you are writing, and the article topic. Then ask for any printed information they have that may be relevant. You might get a thick standard public relations kit, a fact sheet, a list of related organizations, associations, or agencies, a personal response, or a combination of materials. Pictures are also often available. In most cases, this information is free.

Quoting: avoiding plagiarism

No one creates ideas in a vacuum. Every idea is influenced or generated by another idea, yours or one that you've heard or read about. But as a writer, you put a unique spin on an idea, give it a fresh angle, focus, or interpretation that makes it your own. You may use an old idea as a jumping-off place and move in a new direction, or develop the mere seed of an idea from your own experience. When you write an article, the editor expects you to express your ideas in an original way, not simply to rehash those of others. By the same token, it's important to make absolutely clear when you are citing the idea of another speaker or writer and to attribute the statements properly.

Plagiarism is passing off another person's idea as your own. It is probably the most important thing to avoid in writing, both from a legal and an ethical standpoint. Most writers would never deliberately plagiarize another source, but plagiarism can occur by accident, through sloppy note-taking during research. As you take notes during your research, accurately note dates, statistics, and other important facts, and record the source precisely. If you plan to quote a sentence or short passage directly, write down verbatim everything the author says; cite the name of the author, the book or article and publication from which the quote is taken, as well as the date and page number so it can be verified later. Otherwise, summarize the main points in your own words and paraphrase the descriptions of events and concepts. This procedure will not only greatly decrease your chances of unwittingly plagiarizing your source, but will make you more knowledgeable about your subject and take you closer to being ready to draft your article.

Remember that all printed material, computer data bases, video and audio cassettes are protected by copyright law. While you may use a limited amount of quoted material without written permission, the whole subject of "fair use" and what is allowable under this concept has become a highly controversial—and legal—matter, and it is unwise to take any chances with quotations. There is a great deal of material that is no longer protected by copyright, now in what is called "public domain," but you should make sure that what you want to quote even from seemingly old sources is not still in copyright before using it. Of course, even if permission is not required, you *must* cite the writer's, artist's, illustrator's or photographer's name (if available) and the place the material originally appeared.

Your article may require just one method of research or a combination of several. And your research isn't necessarily over when you start to write. But once you get enough material to support your topic, you're ready to start the first draft of your article.

4

Drafting Your Article

You've completed your research, and you are ready to face the blank page or word processor screen. You sit down at your desk and shuffle through your notes. Where do you begin?

Your first try at your article won't be your last. The writing process can be divided into three stages: drafting, revising, and editing. In the draft, you clarify exactly what you want to say. As you draft your article, you work out its organization, its "voice" or style, and elements such as the lead, the conclusion, and supporting facts and anecdotes.

Planning the Structure and Organization

A well-written article has a structure and an organization, so that readers can follow its ideas easily. Before you write the first draft of your article, preparing a simple, informal outline can help you establish its structure. Here is one possible format:

I. Introduction
II. Main point #1
III. Main point #2

IV. Main point #3
V. Conclusion

The following is the outline I used for my article about the wildlife refuge:

> I. Introduction—set the scene, say why I'm visiting the refuge. Define *refuge,* size, and location.
> II. Describe tasks of refuge staff, including methods for counting birds and animals, and establishing restricted areas for rare nesting birds. Discuss purpose of the refuge.
> III. Describe habitat, including vegetation, marshes, salt-water pools and freshwater pools. Discuss how staff helps integrate wildlife and vegetation.
> IV. Describe activities available to visitors, including volunteer work, bird watching, cranberry and plum picking, beachcombing and swimming, surf fishing, clamming, and hunting (!)
> V. Conclusion—end with a vivid description of the *experience* of visiting the refuge for a day, capturing the spirit of the place.

Notice that I divided the article into five main sections: the introduction, three main points, and the conclusion. I then arranged my notes accordingly and began to weed out points and details that were irrelevant to the main theme. I even divided my writing schedule into sections, completing one part of the article at a time. The details of the outline changed after I started writing the draft, but the main structure remained intact, and I knew essentially where I was headed, even though there were surprises for me along the way.

Start with the lead

The lead is the first sentence or paragraph of your article. It's the place where writer and reader meet for the first time. So scribble something down. See what comes out. You can go back and polish it later, but at the outset, putting the lead down on paper gets you into the actual writing of your article.

A good lead is usually short: It hooks readers and reels them right into your article. It may be an anecdote, an exclamation, a question, a direct quote, a challenge to the reader, or a statement of fact, possibly an unusual or startling one. Your lead also sets the tone of the article: formal, informal, funny, poignant, controversial, but one that will be more or less consistent throughout. It often determines whether your readers will keep reading.

Here are a few leads from different published articles:

> If you've ever wanted a '57 Thunderbird, a snazzy little two-seat convertible, now's the time to pick one up cheap.

That is the lead for an article about personal finance, on the best ways to invest small amounts of money. The writer grabs our interest by appealing to two common characteristics of human nature in our society: the fantasy of owning a flashy car and the desire for a bargain. He sets an informal, conversational tone and he implies that he's about to let us in on a secret. We can't help but read further.

Now here is an entirely different kind of lead:

> At some critical point in their lives, many people will become single parents. Some will arrive at this situation through the death of a spouse or mate, while others will go through divorce, unintended pregnancy or adoption. . . . Whatever the pathway to basically unshared parenthood, most single mothers or fathers will find themselves faced

with tremendous financial, physical, and emotional challenges.

The topic of single parenthood is one that currently receives a lot of attention. But this writer hooks the reader in a clever way. She says that "many people" will become single parents. She doesn't just say "women," and she implies that any one of us could find ourselves in this situation. If this statement is true, readers will think, then they'd better find out more about single parenthood. Thus, they will feel inclined to read on.

Finally, here's a lead that hooks readers in another way:

> Just consider the word "sunspace." Doesn't it conjure up a picture of a tropical retreat right in your own home? The plants, the sunshine, the sheer indulgence! As one sunspace manufacturer says, "Have fun dreaming."

It certainly sounds good. This is the lead to an article on home improvement—how homeowners can add a glass-enclosed room such as a conservatory, greenhouse, or solarium to their home. Right away, readers want to know what "sunspace" is, and whether or not they can have it. By using a catchy word—"sunspace"—as well as a direct quote, a question directed at the reader, and images of sunshine, a tropical retreat, dreams and indulgence, the writer catches the readers' attention and makes them want to read the rest of the piece.

As you read published articles, consider the leads carefully. Which ones make you want to read further? Which are boring or just plain turn you off? Reading other writers' leads will help you perfect your own.

Developing your voice

Your writing has a voice that speaks to your readers. It is what makes your writing unique. The voice of any piece of writing is like the tune of a song—the combination of individual notes and rhythms creates the whole melody. Your voice will always be different from anyone else's. In fact, it will differ somewhat from article to article, but as you become more experienced, your voice—your unique style—will become recognizable. So don't try to imitate the voice of another writer; learn to recognize your own.

The voice of a piece of writing also reflects the writer's point of view and conveys the writer's attitude toward the subject, as well as setting the tone of the piece itself, by expressing tension, poignancy, antagonism, humor, fear or sympathy.

The words you choose to express your ideas reveal the voice of your article. Active verbs, specific nouns, and vivid modifiers all contribute to a clear, effective writing voice. Of course, your first draft won't contain your final choice of words; but it will contain the essence of what you want to say, and how you want to say it.

Here is a paragraph from a personal experience article I wrote, about hunting for our first house. Note the choice of words and the tone of the paragraph.

> After listening to us describe the dreary neighborhood we lived in and how we wanted to move out of it, one realtor drove us to a tiny, dirty house on a dirt lot in a dreary neighborhood and told us, "It's perfect for you! It's so cheap!" Another showed us a house with an outhouse—a "charming auxiliary," she called it. When we arrived at a third house, we noticed fist-sized holes punched in most of the walls and

doors. "I don't know what happened here," the realtor said sweetly, "but it was a particularly nasty divorce."

The informal language, direct quotes, and descriptions of the houses all contribute to the voice of the article: humor with an edge. Words such as "dreary," "dirty," and "cheap" as well as the choice of quotes help set the scene and convey the attitude toward the subject. All of these factors combine to create the voice of the piece; another writer probably would have written about house hunting in an entirely different manner.

Facts, anecdotes, and quotations

Readers love facts, concrete numbers and percentages, statistics and unusual bits of information, but they also like to read about people. Thus, a lively article that combines facts and anecdotes—brief stories or descriptions of incidents or events involving people—is bound to catch your readers' attention. In the personal experience article on our house search, I included examples or anecdotes of the houses we saw and realtors we met. I quoted the realtors, which helped make the story more immediate, effective, and humorous. In my article about the wildlife refuge, I presented facts about the different populations of wildlife:

> The refuge will serve as a stopover for nearly 6,000 geese on their trip south this fall; 300 of them will stay, wintering over. Wood ducks, black ducks, mallards, pintails and shovellers all call Plum Island home. About 70 deer roam the refuge, although there have been no reports of Lyme disease.

Then I recounted an anecdote about the interaction between hunters and birds:

[There was a] particular hunting problem of several years ago. Hunters were allowed to shoot from the state reservation located at the southern tip of the island, and some of the shot dropped into Stage Island Pool. Canada geese, in rooting through the pool for food, swallowed the shot and suffered lead poisoning.

The combination of facts and anecdotes helps to paint the complete picture.

When you use direct quotes, do so sparingly, and don't substitute them for your own ideas; and never represent another person's words as your own. Simply use quotations as you would seasoning in a good meal.

Endings

Your ending is as important as your lead; it should leave the reader with a sense of satisfaction. The ending doesn't necessarily answer all the questions, but it sends the reader away feeling that the piece is complete. A satisfactory ending can be achieved in a variety of ways: offering advice, asking a question, describing a final scene, or giving a personal impression. But a really good ending adds a slight twist, an element of the unexpected that still seems "right" in the context of the article. The article on personal finance concludes by offering advice to readers seeking professional financial help:

> So shop around; then find an individual counselor you like and feel comfortable with. Remember, this person will know more about you and your money than your closest friend.

In this ending, the writer also makes an unexpected, but useful, point in offering advice that readers will remember after they have put away the magazine. The writer of the article on single parenthood ended her article by juxtaposing the health of single parents with the availability of cheap oil, and achieved the surprise of recognition:

> With the current backlash against the homeless and the advent of the frightening term "compassion fatigue," we need to extend ourselves in some significant way. Surely the physical and emotional health of our own mothers, fathers, and children is as important as the availability of cheap oil.

The writer calls on readers to take action, even if it is simply to be aware of the difficult task of being a single parent. Note that both endings have that extra "punch" of surprise.

As you read published articles, pay attention to the endings. Which leave you satisfied? Which just fizzle? As you draft your own articles, give as much attention to your endings as you do to your leads. Then you'll be on your way to the next step in your article: revising and editing.

When you have finished a draft of your article, put it away for a while to give it time to "cool"—overnight or longer, if possible. Then, when you are ready to revise, both you and your manuscript will be fresh.

5

Revising and Editing

Expect to revise. Revision doesn't mean that your draft isn't good, but that your article isn't finished yet. "Revision isn't failure," notes an experienced writer. "It's an essential part of the process."

Nor is revision the same as editing; it is much more than that. Revising involves "re-seeing" the whole piece: its focused idea, its structure, its voice, its details—not that you must radically change any or all of these elements. Rather, it means that you examine them all afresh, with a critical eye.

The Revision Process

First read your article all the way through, keeping in mind your focused idea. Does the piece stick to the main point you want to make, or does it wander? If it wanders, read the article again to determine why. Is the point of view strong? Do the facts, anecdotes, and quotations support the central idea? Finally, does the piece contain enough information to warrant an entire article dealing with the focused idea? If the answer is "no" to any of these questions, consider whether you need to strengthen the point of view, choose new supporting details, or add more information. If any or all of these options still do not do the trick, perhaps you need to change the angle somewhat.

Structure and voice

Since the structure of your article is the frame on which it is built, you need to make sure it is solid. As you read your article again, ask yourself what your readers want to know and at what point in the article they need to know it. Is the information presented in a logical sequence? If you are describing steps in a process, do they follow each other in correct sequence? Is each paragraph cohesive, with a natural transition into the next? Do supporting facts, anecdotes, and quotations appear where they belong, or would they be more effective if they were moved? If necessary, shift elements—sentences, phrases, or words—so the piece will be clear and convincing.

Once you have the main points and their supporting paragraphs in logical order, consider the transitions. Do you lead the reader smoothly from one point to the next? Words such as *but, and,* and *although* help to signal transitions.

How does your article sound? Does it flow as if you were speaking naturally to another person? Or does it shift back and forth between humor and seriousness, between formal and informal language? Your article should sound as if one person is speaking, not several.

Ask yourself again for whom you are writing and what is your main point. Do the words express what you want to say clearly? Are they appropriate for the readers you want to reach? If not, reword any passages to reflect the voice you want the reader to "hear." Use informal language if a more casual style fits the subject and tone of the article; or snap your readers to attention with some short, crisp sentences to communicate your ideas more clearly and forcibly.

Your voice is closely linked to style, which is the unique combination of words you choose to convey your meaning. In your first draft, you chose words designed to express your ideas as clearly as possible; now it's time to polish the language with specific, active words that appeal to the senses.

Nouns and verbs are the strongest words available to you. Adjectives and adverbs are the trimmings on a package of substance. Learn to use specific nouns and precise verbs to express your ideas and avoid the passive voice whenever possible. If you appeal to your readers' senses—sight, sound, smell, taste, and touch—they will experience what you have experienced. Consider the following passage from a first-person travel piece I wrote:

> We arrived in Kathmandu after a two-day flight, weary but eager to meet our guide and the rest of the climbing team and get off to the mountains. It was the middle of the Festival of Light, and fireworks burst through the darkness, children banged pots and pans as they marched along the dirt streets, shopkeepers lit candles in their windows, and sacred Hindu cows wandered among the shadows, nuzzling heaps of garbage for morsels of food. Dogs yowled through the night and rickshaws clattered back and forth.

Notice the verbs *burst, banged, nuzzling, yowled,* and *clattered*. Each of these describes precisely a sound or movement. The nouns *fireworks, morsels,* and *rickshaws* describe objects that can be seen, tasted or smelled, and heard. Modifiers such as *weary, eager,* and *sacred* clarify the scene further. Thus, I tried to put readers who have not been to Kathmandu right beside me on a walk through the streets at night.

Pay close attention to the rhythm created by the length and structure of your sentences. You can pile up a number of short sentences to produce an effect; but then slip in a longer sentence or two for a change of pace. Sentences of unvarying length and structure can have a hypnotic effect on your reader.

Fresh figures of speech are a delightful surprise for the reader; clichés, unless they are direct quotes or used to make a specific point, imply that you are a lazy writer. Creating new figures of speech is actually fun; and you'll find that they express your thoughts more accurately. In describing a promising young political candidate, don't use the cliché, "She's as sharp as a tack." Instead, create a new expression that describes the woman more precisely: "She's as sharp as the point on her fountain pen."

Details, leads, and endings

Once you feel that the structure and voice are right for your article, you can have fun with the details. In your first draft, you started to include details by presenting facts, anecdotes, and quotations. Now it's time to flesh them out.

First, consider the level of detail that is required to communicate successfully with your audience. In an article on kayaks, will your readers expect you to include the measurements a boat builder uses in designing a single-person sea kayak? Or would they be more interested in knowing where they can paddle in the new kayak they've just bought? This is important, whether you are writing for a general publication (in which readers want less technical detail and more general background information) or for a specialized publication (in which readers already have background knowledge and are looking for more in-depth, technical information). At this point, it is also a good idea to go back and study the publication for which you are writing.

Next, analyze your article to see whether any of the main points need to be underscored with further details. Do you make any claims that aren't supported by facts, statements from authorities or experts, or description? If so, tackle these elements first, and add specifics to back up general statements. If you can't verify a statement, delete it.

Examine the main points and information again to see where you can add a detail that brings the idea to life. If you are writing a profile, add details about your subject's appearance and surroundings. If you are explaining how to build a chair from a kit, describe the subtle glow of the finished rocker. If you are writing about gardening, note the delicate scents and brilliant colors of particular flowers.

Just as you may make substantial revisions in the body of your article, you should do the same for your lead and ending. Don't feel so committed to the original lead or ending that you neglect to polish or change it as you revise. If the lead or ending doesn't fit your final, revised draft, the whole effect of your article will be weakened.

Choosing a title

You can choose a title at any point in the process of drafting and revising an article. If you do so before beginning the first draft, by the time you're almost finished you may find that the working title doesn't really apply. In that case, you must alter it or come up with an entirely new one. A good title, like a good lead, captures the reader's attention at once. It's quite possible that the editor will change your title, but you have to give him or her something to work with.

Choose a title that focuses on the main point or unique approach of your story. Be clever, not cute. Take a look at a few titles:

> "Unraveling Cable" (how to choose a cable television service)
> "Boots That Warm Your Soles" (states clearly what the article is about, but uses a pun)
> "Single Again (and Smarter This Time)" (about re-entering the dating world)
> "Designer Beef" (about pampered cattle that are bred for healthier, more nutritious beef)

Each of these titles piques reader interest by using a play on words and/or stating succinctly what the article is about.

Finally, don't get hooked on revision. At some point, you'll need to let go of the manuscript and send it off. There is no such thing as a perfect piece of writing; but you know when you have reached the point at which you have given your best effort to your article. Decide when you've come to that point and stop.

Editing and Proofreading

You are now ready for the final editing and proofreading (what I call the "red-pencil stage"). Use the following tips as an editing checklist. If you aren't certain about rules of usage, spelling, or grammar, consult a handbook or dictionary. Experienced writers keep their dictionaries and grammar handbooks within arm's reach at all times. No one is infallible when it comes to spelling, grammar, and usage, so the professional writer makes the extra effort to find and correct errors.

1. Read your article closely and carefully for clarity. Does each sentence say exactly what you mean? Have you chosen precise and effective words to express your ideas?
2. Be sure that you've been consistent in the tense of your verbs, and that verbs agree with their subjects.
3. Wherever possible, replace passive voice with active voice. It is much more exciting to read about someone *doing* something than about something *being done* to a person. For example, the following sentence is in passive voice:

This fresh fish market is visited by scores of tourists.

Note how much stronger the sentence becomes when it is recast in active voice:
Scores of tourists visit this fresh fish market.

4. Make sure that all pronouns have clear antecedents. Your readers need to know whom you are talking about when you use *he, she, it, they, them,* and other pronouns. Be sure also that pronouns agree in person, number, and gender with their antecedents.

To proofread your article, read slowly, word for word. Use the following tips as a proofreading checklist:

1. Make sure your use of punctuation is correct.
2. Check for correct capitalization.

3. Note correct use of quotation marks, underlining, and numerals.

4. Be sure all words are spelled correctly. Use your dictionary! If you have a computer program with a spelling checker on it, use it carefully. But always remember, *it is no substitute for proofreading.* These programs don't catch dropped or repeated words, typos, homophones (words such as *to/too/two* and *rain/rein/reign,* which sound the same but are spelled differently and have totally different meanings), or words that are spelled correctly but for which the meaning is wrong in this particular context (*sullen/sudden, start/stare, grape/gripe*).

Preparing Your Final Manuscript

Type (or retype) the final manuscript on a typewriter or word processor, always using double spacing on standard white 8½" × 11" paper (no onionskin). Avoid using a dot matrix computer printer unless it is near letter quality; it is very hard to read, and most editors will not accept it. If the editor wants several copies, you can photocopy a good typed copy. Make sure to keep a copy for yourself. Type your name, address, and phone number in the upper lefthand corner of the first page of the article. Center the title of your article a few lines below. Manuscript pages should be numbered at the top of each page and attached with a paper clip (do not use staples). Some writers like to place their last name at the top corner of every page; this is helpful if a page gets misplaced at the publication.

Now proofread your final, typewritten article, sentence by sentence, word by word. If you find any errors, it is O.K. to pencil in a few small changes in your final version—like adding or deleting an apostrophe or comma, transposing two letters, inserting or cutting a word or two—before sending it to the editor. But if you need to make more than one or two minor changes, it's better to take the time to retype the page or make a new printout of it to give the manuscript a professional look.

After proofreading, make the necessary copies of your article (either have it photocopied or run off an extra copy on your computer printer). Then write a short cover letter to the editor, saying that your article (give the title and topic) is enclosed. If you have agreed to provide illustrations, wrap them carefully and include them with the manuscript. Insert your article and cover letter in a manila envelope (never use a letter-size envelope that necessitates folding the article unless your article is only a few pages long).

When you mail your article, don't guess at the correct postage; have the package weighed at the post office or use a postal scale. (You don't want your article to arrive on the editor's desk with postage due!) First-class mail is sufficient; there is no need to send your article registered, certified, or express unless the editor has made a special request. After you have mailed your manuscript, relax. But don't think your job is over. There may be more to do!

Outside Editing

Give the editor at least six to eight weeks to consider your article. The editor's priority is always the issue of the magazine or newspaper that is due out next. You may enclose a self-addressed, stamped postcard with your submission, asking the editor to indicate that the manuscript was received and when. But if you don't have any word after two months, you may drop the editor a polite note.

If the editor asks you to rewrite some parts of your article or transpose some sentences, paragraphs, or words, don't be offended. You should, in fact, be encouraged. Your job is to give the editor the article needed for publication, and it doesn't mean that you've done a bad job if you need to make some changes. Of course you've put a lot of work into your piece, but no article is perfect, and a professional writer knows how to accept suggestions for rewrites or revisions. Ask the editor what specific changes are required, and if there is a deadline for the rewrite.

Even after you make the requested changes, your accepted article usually will be edited by a copy editor, often a different editor from the one with whom you have been dealing. Copy editing may include some final tightening and smoothing out of the prose; it also includes corrections in spelling, grammar, usage, punctuation, mechanics, use of numerals, etc. Each publication has a standard style of capitalization, abbreviation, and hyphenation that it follows for consistency, and in most cases, you will not be consulted on these decisions. You may or may not see the edited version before publication, depending on the policy of the magazine or newspaper.

Now you wait to see your article in print. When you finally hold the publication in your hands, you know you're a published writer. And no matter how many articles you write in the future, you'll always experience a feeling of satisfaction and accomplishment that comes with seeing the finished piece on the printed page.

Article Types

6

PERSONAL EXPERIENCE

THE PERSONAL EXPERIENCE ARTICLE draws on your feelings (or those of someone you know), impressions, perceptions, and emotional reactions to an event or an experience. In the personal experience article, you relate an event through your senses and thoughts. This type of article doesn't usually need to be researched (except for specific facts, names, dates, etc.), and it may also be relatively short—usually 1,000 words or fewer.

ELEMENTS AND TYPES

A personal experience article can be serious or funny, and can deal with any number of subjects. However, the idea must be original, or offer a new angle on a familiar subject. "I get a lot of columns on class reunions, childhood Christmases, Mother's and Father's Day, or a child's first day of school," remarks a newspaper editor who publishes a weekly first-person column open to free-lance writers. These are generally rejected in favor of articles on commuting, income taxes, house hunting, step-family relationships, recycling, and homelessness—as long as they relate to personal experience and have a strong viewpoint.

Point of view is extremely important in personal experience articles. Although this type of article need not be just your own story it recounts some aspects of your own experience. Your purpose and goal may be to entertain, instruct, move your readers to action, or to help them cope with a similar situation: dealing with a parent's Alzheimer's disease, for example, or offering a fresh view on the importance of a community sex education program. Whatever your point of view and purpose in writing a personal experience article, it must be readable.

The language you use in a personal experience article should be concise and clear, describing events and ideas in as few words as possible, engaging the emotions of the readers, but without sentimentality. Omit any unnecessary details. Make sure that your lead and ending establish the situation and wrap it up quickly, with your point clearly made.

Language sets the tone and mood of a personal experience piece, and may be what ultimately sells it to an editor and readers. You aren't just presenting facts here; sometimes you must convey your own private thoughts and feelings, describe a painful experience, or even expose a secret (or "vice") about yourself. The words you choose make the difference between a successful and an unsuccessful article.

Finally, even though you may be writing about a personal matter, it is essential that you achieve some detachment. Remember that you are writing for others, not just for yourself. Put yourself in their shoes and share the experience in a way readers can relate to and identify with emotionally. Your readers don't care so much how *you* feel about an issue as they do about how you make *them* feel. One of the best ways to achieve this is to give your personal experience article time to "cool" after you've written it. When you revise it later on, you'll read the manuscript with a more critical eye.

Here is a brief, 300-word personal experience piece that I wrote for the Living Forum of *The Boston Globe:*

Nothing Like Going for the Gold

For most of my life, I've dreamed of winning a gold medal at the Olympics. When I was 8, I thought I'd be a ski champion. When I was 12, I began to ride horses in earnest. Riding consumed my life for years. So, when I fantasize about my gold medal, I am always astride a tall, glossy bay thoroughbred clearing the final fence in the stadium jumping event, to the roar of the crowd.

Sometimes, dreams change. I haven't been to the Olympics, but there is a 20,000-foot-high mountain in Nepal whose summit I have reached. Climbing in the Himalayas is lonely and exhausting, and there is no one there to cheer for you. There are no judges of style and no medals awarded for grabbing the peak first. It is unglamorous in the extreme. But standing on the hard snow of the summit, surrounded by the deep and unrelenting silence of the Himalayas was for me equal to hearing the thunderous applause of the Olympic crowd.

Dreams don't just come true; we make them happen. Several weeks ago, I went to see my brother, Andy, compete in the Bud Light endurance triathlon on Cape Cod. Five hundred athletes struggled to swim 2½ miles in the ocean, ride their bikes 112 miles, then run a full marathon of 26 miles.

A few of those athletes competed to win. Some competed to qualify for others races or to improve previous times. Andy entered to finish. For more than 12 hours, he stretched himself to his limit, then staggered across the line in the dark, the winner of his own dream. And a dream is a wonderful thing to win; for it is almost always something we once thought was out of reach.

Note that the piece deals with a single idea, building to its point at the very end. Events and details are presented sparingly, each one relating to the main point. And I reveal a secret about myself: my dream about participating in the Olympics. While most readers are not triathletes or mountaineers, everyone has dreams. My intention in writing this piece was to validate the point that dreams are important, worth pursuing, and even achievable.

Humor

Personal experience articles may fall into one of two subcategories—humor or commentary—and in fact, even these sometimes overlap, for commentary can be humorous.

You don't have to be a comedian to write humor. Humor combines surprise with recognition of a truth. Humor pieces show the funny side of everyday life, whether it's buying a car, sending a child to college, or looking for a job.

If you start out with a humorous lead, make sure that you can sustain the humor and mood throughout the piece without forcing it. And be certain that your humor won't be offensive to readers. While laughter is good medicine, keep your humor within the bounds of good taste.

Opinion and commentary

Check the op-ed page of your local newspaper, and you're almost sure to see at least one piece of commentary by a free-lance writer. Opinion or commentary pieces are short, to-the-point essays that express the writer's view of different aspects of life. Topics may range from national politics and issues to local environmental or educational concerns, but they all share one thing: timeliness. Timing is particularly important in opinion pieces; yesterday's commentary is no more valuable (or salable) than yesterday's news.

The personal opinion piece should not be too technical; if you are writing about economics, you should be able to relate it to your own as well as your readers' pocketbooks. In addition, your opinion should be expressed in a concrete, objective way—that is, its style isn't ranting and raving, hurling insults, or hand-wringing. Instead, this type of short article uses examples from personal experience to make a point. Commentary expresses *opinions* and deals with social and political issues more directly than does the more general personal experience article.

SUBMISSIONS

The personal experience article is a good vehicle by which beginning free-lance writers can become published writers. Literally thousands of newspapers and magazines publish such articles by free-lance writers. Local newspapers as well as national magazines, such as *Newsweek* (in a section called "My Turn," for free-lance writers) are viable markets. But remember to study several issues of a publication thoroughly before submitting your manuscript.

The personal experience article is the one type of article that does not require a query. Rather, it's the writing style, point of view, and tone of the finished article that are its main selling points. Writing a query for a humor piece just wouldn't work, because the humor itself is a key element to the article. So write and polish your personal experience article, and then send the completed manuscript off to an editor. Follow the guidelines in Chapter 5 for preparing and mailing manuscripts, and make sure to include a self-addressed, stamped envelope with your submission. And don't be discouraged by rejections. You are, after all, submitting an unsolicited manuscript, and the editor may have to decline your piece for any number of reasons. If it is rejected, just submit it to another publication.

The personal experience article not only gives you the opportunity to build up publishing credits, it also offers you entry to a publication for which you may write a longer article in the future.

7

ROUND-UPS

ROUND-UPS ARE SHORT PIECES that round up facts and opinions about a subject. A round-up is based on interview responses to a single theme or question: "What is the most romantic restaurant in New York City?" "How did you spend your first Thanksgiving in a new home or town?" "What makes marriage successful (or unsuccessful)?" "Should sex education be taught at the elementary school level?" The round-up writer comes up with the question, interviews people for a variety of answers, and ties the responses together in a lively, cohesive article. A round-up can be a good way for you to get published; it can also give you the opportunity to prove your skills to an editor who might want you to write a longer, more substantive article about the subject later on.

To get ideas for round-up articles, read newspapers, magazines, and advertisements; watch television; listen to the radio; listen to what your friends and relatives talk about. A good round-up question is one that is specific but provocative and open-ended, allowing for unique or surprising responses. Your round-up question can be serious—"When did you realize that you were an alcoholic?"—or light-hearted—"Who makes the best pizza in town?" Your question can tie in with current social or political issues: "Should your town spend the necessary money to start a recycling program?" "How do you feel about the drug rehabilitation center that is being established on your street?" "Do you think aging parents are better cared for by their children or by a nursing home?" Your question can be designed to elicit responses about personal matters: "Who has been the most influential person in your life?" "How has having children affected your marriage?" "How did you cope when a parent (or other loved one) died of suicide?" Most round-up questions require that you interview people with something specific in common—say, a group of suicide survivors or children who are considering how to care for aging parents, or people with the same occupation, such as police officers or teachers, or people who share a common interest or hobby, such as photography or gardening.

Other round-up questions require only that interviewees live in the same town, or are aware of a particular issue. A nearby college, town meeting, shopping mall, historical society gathering, public demonstration, or rally can provide you with ample opportunity to collar people with your round-up question. Sometimes, you may be able to interview celebrities by approaching their representatives (a good source for this is *The Celebrity Phone Book,* by Scott Siegel and Barbara Siegel, published by New American Library/Plume). Interviews for a round-up will usually be much shorter and much less formal than those for most other types of articles. Even when you simply approach some people on the street or in a public place, be sure to ask for permission to quote them by name. Many round-up articles just refer to those questioned as "a man," "a woman," "a college student," "a housewife," or whatever.

A round-up isn't just a string of facts or quotes. Although the question itself provides a framework for the article, you must construct a coherent article from your own introduction and transitions along with the responses you received to your questions. You may find that one person's response leads smoothly to another's; or that juxtaposing two opposing viewpoints provides good contrast and heightened interest for your article. In either case, you'll need to use effective transition sentences, and perhaps even provide some background information, particularly if the question deals with an issue with which readers may not be completely familiar. In addition, you may want to include some introductory comments about your interviewees, such as occupation or town of residence.

A round-up on how couples keep love and romance alive introduced its interviewees just enough to give readers some perspective on their comments:

> A male college junior theorizes, "Love is feeling crazy about another person. First you feel that physical attraction, and then you notice all the hidden things about that person."
> ... A young male engineer acknowledges, "Romance keeps the fountain flowing. It's that special ingredient that adds sparkle and refreshment to the life-giving waters of love. Without romance, the water can become flat or brackish." ...
> A middle-aged wife, mother and teacher declares, "Love is not desperate, but thrives on humor, ordinary experiences and relaxed moments. Romance is all the extra, sometimes silly things you do to keep love playful and eternally young."

Leads and endings are just as important in the round-up as they are in other types of articles. The round-up on love and romance began this way:

> Fast and furious, hot and heavy, pell-mell and passionate. These alliterative couplings might well have described love in the liberated, liberal '60s and '70s. Readily available birth control, especially the pill, facilitated the consummation of desire . . . but wait a minute! Suddenly the environment is in, and conspicuous consumption is out. Overworked, "double shift" women have found out that "having it all" can mean "doing it all." Real estate is in a slump, [we're] in a recession, and the United States is at war. Can love and marriage survive in these hard, discouraging times? This week, in honor of Valentine's Day, we talked with a sociologist, a professional writer of love letters, a couple married for 57 years, and with numerous people in the street. Yes, love still springs eternal, but the pump requires priming.

You might want to end your round-up with a paragraph stating your own conclusions about the subject, or you might choose to end with a particularly incisive, funny or poignant quote by one of your interviewees.

Of course, you should study any publication you plan to query for your round-up, first to be sure that they publish round-up articles, and second to determine what types of round-up questions editors prefer. In your query to an editor, make your round-up question absolutely clear. Offer some background information on the topic, and some tantalizing facts. Tell your editor where and how you plan to go about getting answers, and if you have any well-known people whose answers would be pertinent and whom you know you can reach, mention their names.

8

How-To or Service Articles

A SERVICE ARTICLE TELLS THE reader how to do something and/or where to do it, whether it's taking a trip, building a piece of furniture, or planting a perennial garden. This type of article carefully defines terms and provides all the details a reader needs to complete the project or reach the destination.

Though you don't have to be an expert or a specialist in a field to write a publishable service article, an editor will expect you to cover your subject authoritatively. To accomplish this, you should know enough about your topic to ask the right questions in an interview, focus your research on the points you need to verify, and in your article answer the questions readers would be likely to ask, so they can follow your directions with no difficulty.

Service pieces require varying amounts of research, depending on the level of detail you plan to include in the article, how much you already know about the topic, and the type of reader you are writing for. For example, if you are planning to write a short article on how to repair a flat bicycle tire, you won't need to do much more than review the steps. But if you are writing a piece on making business travel easy, you'll want to interview experienced business travelers as well as travel agents, and perhaps even airline or car rental employees. Of course, if you intend to write even a short article on a topic that involves health care or safety (such as how to treat severe sunburn), you should consult a medical expert to be sure your information and advice are accurate.

The structure of a how-to article falls naturally into sequential steps. Thus, it's helpful to make an outline of the main steps of the process you are going to describe, then fill in the "blanks" of the outline with necessary information and background facts. For a craft article or a piece on home repair, for instance, it is valuable to include a list of necessary supplies and equipment at the beginning. Use subheads to divide the process into manageable steps or stages.

Service pieces often have sidebars—with lists of safety tips, names and addresses of hotels or shops, hints for packing, or suggestions for easy clean-up after a project. As you plan your article, consider whether a sidebar might be effective or useful. (You can suggest a sidebar and what you plan to include in your query.)

The level of detail in a service article depends largely on the audience. If you are explaining to a general audience how to weave a simple basket, you'll concentrate on simple, basic terms and techniques. But if your article is intended for experienced crafters, you can gloss over what you may assume they already know and focus on the advanced or more intricate techniques of weaving.

Regardless of your personal experience with a subject,

the extent of your research, and how much detail is required for your audience, your service article must cover every step and define every term accurately and in proper sequence. If you are describing a process that you know well, it's easy to overlook a step. So once you have drafted your article and let it "cool" for a while, read through it as if you intend to complete the process yourself. Better yet, give the article to a knowledgeable outsider to determine whether you have answered all the how-to and where-to questions a reader will have.

A service article should present the facts in a clear, concise style, without unnecessary digressions or description. Since your aim is to teach the readers how to do something, you should convey enthusiasm for the subject, using precise words that will appeal to their senses and make them "catch the fever" for your subject. Here, for example, is how the opening paragraph of an article on how to build furniture might read:

> Picture yourself serving Thanksgiving dinner to your entire family on a dining room table that you have built by yourself. Imagine your guests lounging in rich, elegant chairs crafted in cherry, rubbed to a deep, glossy patina by your own hands. You can make this fantasy come true, even with a tight budget. With a few tools and some elbow grease, you can build beautiful furniture from kits.

Notice that this paragraph engages the reader by showing that he or she can have elegant furniture even on a tight budget and without being trained as a carpenter, by building the furniture from kits. The article would then turn to the details that the reader needs to tackle these projects. The language is precise, so the reader can easily follow the process:

To begin, choose a spot in your home that is well lit and well ventilated, and provides you with enough space to assemble your piece of furniture. If you don't have a regular workbench, it's a good idea to spread a drop cloth on the floor, covering the area on which you plan to work. Open the kit and take out the instructions as well as the list of tools, parts, and materials. Read the instructions thoroughly. Then check each item in the box against the list of parts and materials to be sure that everything has been included and that no piece is damaged or defective. Group your tools in a single area, such as a corner of the drop cloth, so that you can get your hands on them easily. Now you're ready to build your masterpiece!

The article would proceed from here, explaining step by step how to assemble and finish the piece of furniture. It might also include a sidebar that lists names and addresses of companies that sell high-quality furniture kits, seconds or discounted kits, or kits for particular styles of furniture.

Editors welcome service articles from beginners and established writers alike, as long as the writer presents a compelling query that demonstrates familiarity with the publication's audience and some knowledge of the subject. In fact, I launched my free-lance writing career with a service article: a how-to, where-to piece on backcountry skiing that I sold to the travel section of the Sunday *New York Times*.

For an article that describes a process, your query should list its main steps (here's where the bulleted list in the query format presented in Chapter 2 comes in especially handy). For an article that tells readers where to go for an activity, list some of the most important places you plan to cover.

If you think that a few simple illustrations—graphs, drawings or photos—would strengthen your article, mention this in your query, or offer to collaborate with someone who is a professional artist or photographer; or offer to provide rough sketches that the editor can turn over to a staff artist for final drawings. The success of your article should not depend on elaborate drawings or color photographs. Your prose *should* be able to tell the whole story by itself.

9

PROFILES

"PEOPLE LIKE TO read about people," says a writer who specializes in writing profiles. A profile centers on an individual because she or he is "famous," unique, unusual, or has made an important contribution to or discovery or invention in a particular field. But the profile does more than simply describe the person: It puts him or her in the context of society in a way that captures the interest and attention of a wide readership.

If you are considering writing a profile of a man or woman either in your own local or regional area, or someone whose achievement has had wider implications and impact, ask yourself why. What makes this person intriguing and interesting to you and to prospective readers? Has she or he overcome difficult odds to achieve an important goal? Or accomplished something inspiring or unique? Is the person controversial or famous; if so, why? For example, in a profile of a woman who is a forest firefighter, you might include details of her struggle to gain the recognition and trust of her male superiors and colleagues; readers most certainly will want to know how she succeeds. Reading about another person's struggles, failures, achievements, and methods of coping can be inspiring or simply entertaining.

A successful profile is largely dependent upon an in-person interview. While you should plan the interview with your subject as outlined in Chapter 3, a profile interview may require more time. Also, it is important for you as a writer to note and absorb the details of your subject's surroundings, appearance, mannerisms, voice, gestures, and general attitude. Is he or she friendly, withdrawn, aloof, forthcoming, imperious?

Schedule your interview in an appropriate setting. For example, if your subject is a commercial fisherman (and that is the point of the interview and profile you are planning to write), try to conduct the interview aboard his or her boat, on the dock, or somewhere near his workplace.

Your profile should include details that create an overall impression of the person. I once wrote a profile of a couple who spent their honeymoon on a three-week kayak trip. I introduced them to readers this way:

> Brian Kologe didn't spend his honeymoon beneath the spray of Niagara Falls. Nor did he relax on the sunny deck of a Carnival Cruise ship. But he did spend it on the water. In July 1988, two weeks after Brian and his wife, Anne Spraker, were married, they launched their heavy-sea kayak into Penobscot Bay for a three-week journey north to Eastport, Maine.
>
> Now, a year later, Brian and Anne talk about kayaking together with laughter and tenderness, sometimes from different points of view. Early in their relationship, they tried canoeing together, but fought over who was steering where. Two years before they married, they bought the kayak.

Physical details, such as hair color and height, also add to the picture, especially if the person has somewhat unusual characteristics—bright red hair, bushy eyebrows, or especially long, painted fingernails. Age tells readers something about the person, but you should state this only if your subject agrees. (You can always convey the approximate age by saying that he or she is "fortyish.") Mannerisms and gestures, voice, and speech patterns further help the reader visualize the person. Perhaps your subject leans forward as he talks, runs his fingers through his hair, or keeps his eyes averted, never making eye contact. All of these details help your readers visualize and come to feel they know your subject.

Anecdotes create drama, and the interview is the place to get them. Frame some of your questions in a way that will lead your interviewee to relate some anecdotes that will help you bring him or her to life for your readers. Don't just pile anecdotes one on top of the other. Choose a few of the most revealing.

Dialogue adds immediacy to a profile; it lets your subject speak to the reader in his or her own words. As with anecdotes, use dialogue selectively and purposefully; it is, after all, your article, not a speech being made by your subject. In my profile of the two kayakers, I used a combination of anecdotes and dialogue to develop drama and immediacy, as well as to illustrate the relationship between these two people:

> The most ambitious trip they made recently was on Memorial Day weekend, when they paddled from Amesbury to Marblehead. After leaving a car in Marblehead, they returned to Amesbury and stuffed the kayak with camping supplies and food (couscous, soup, canned tuna, fruit, cookies and tea) and launched straight into bad weather.

"We knew something was coming up," Brian recalls. They pulled into Essex Bay just as a squall blew across the water, driving wind and rain around their small boat.

Desperate to escape the storm, "we went up one of the marsh creeks to a sheltered place," Anne says. "The tide was low enough that our heads were below ground."

"We just sat there for about an hour and drank tea," Brian remembers. In this case, experience counted. On this trip, they knew how to handle a squall; they'd encountered a bad one on the honeymoon journey.

Occasionally, you may want to interview other people—friends, family, or colleagues of your profile subject—to gain a different perspective of the person. Before doing so, however, ask your subject's permission. Then write or call the other people and proceed as you would with a regular interview.

Do your best to present a balanced view of the person, even someone who is considered controversial. No person is all good, all bad, all funny, or all brilliant. We all have our quirks and inconsistencies, strengths and weaknesses. It is this mixture that makes people complex, interesting, intriguing—and worth reading about.

As is the case with most other types of articles, the profile requires a query to show the editor why his or her audience would be interested in an article about the person you've chosen. Including in your query and sample paragraphs an anecdote or two about the subject of your profile will bring him or her to life for the editor. Your bulleted list can include achievements, controversies, unique accomplishments, and other intriguing information. Also be sure to tell the editor what relationship you have, if any, with the person about whom you want to write the profile. Are you personally acquainted? Is he or she a relative, friend, or colleague? If you do not know your subject personally, how do you plan to reach him or her? Do you anticipate any difficulties in gaining access to the person?

It is rarely, if ever, advisable to let your profile subject read a copy of your manuscript before you submit it for publication. While in most cases doing so would present no problems, if your profile is of a controversial figure, or you have included details that are less than flattering, you may be asked to cut or change statements. It is well, therefore, to discuss this in advance with the subject and your editor. In agreeing to be interviewed for a profile, and to discuss various matters with you, the subject has also agreed that you will write an article about him or her. It is your job as a writer to present as fair, balanced, and truthful a picture of the person as possible—not to flatter him or her at the expense of accuracy.

It may be that sometimes having the subject read the article helps, by clarifying a statement or pointing out an error of fact. But most writers will not and should not agree to such advance reading.

10

FEATURE ARTICLES

FEATURES ARE THE MAIN ARTICLES that appear in magazines and newspapers. These are usually the longest articles, are often accompanied by illustrations, and occupy a prominent position in the publication. This is the type of article that most free-lance writers aspire to because it gives the most recognition and pays the highest rates.

Subject areas for features run the gamut from diet programs to homelessness to solar energy to divorce. They may include an analysis of the success or failure of certain diets; how teachers deal with homeless students; and current uses of solar energy for the average household.

Because of its prominence, length, and depth, a feature requires more research than other types of articles, usually drawing upon a variety of research sources: personal interviews, letter writing, as well as primary and secondary sources. A feature article may require some travel for research (but don't expect the publication to pay for this unless the editor agreed to it in advance). Only established professionals are likely to be given travel allowances by a major magazine or newspaper.

Although a feature article is longer and more detailed than other types of articles, it should not be a full-length account of personal experience *unless* the point of the article is based on the personal experience, as for instance, a trek across Tibet or the problems, perils, and pleasures of starting a bed-and-breakfast business. And the feature must reveal the writer's viewpoint.

Features often make extensive use of anecdotes, case histories, and testimony from experts, all of which help relate information to human experience. Readers will absorb the information you've garnered from your research much more easily when it's presented in the context of real-life experiences. For a feature on the challenges that single parents face, one free-lance writer interviewed a number of single fathers and mothers and used case histories like the following to develop the personal side of the article:

> "Jeanne," a bright, hard-working professional woman [and single parent] with a decent salary, still finds herself in a financial quagmire at the end of each month. After she left a long-term, unsatisfactory relationship, she had to begin again from scratch. With no extended family to offer even temporary help, she experienced the agony and humiliation of being hounded by angry creditors. Now, with a bad credit rating, she is faced with the usual black hole of apartment rental, a car that has well over 100,000 miles, and a child with excellent grades who is almost ready for college.
>
> Jeanne says, "I have a responsible position, one that requires a reliable car. Most of my peers are men who own homes and cars that run. But what is worse, my teen-age daughter is very much in touch with my work, my hours, my

bills and my problems. I worry that she is not free to act as a normal kid. She worries that I will miss her when she goes to college."

Fortunately, Jeanne has sought counseling for herself and her daughter. She concludes, "You pay big and your family pays if you decide to date and go out. And there is rivalry when you bring someone home. If you try to maintain a private social life, your children will be neglected in ways that a married couple's children would not. Still, the drive to be loved, needed and heard sometimes takes priority. The drive to share the small details of your day with a caring adult is an undeniably strong drive that equals the parenting drive."

Of course a case history is longer and more fully developed than a brief anecdote or quote, making it more appropriate for the feature article than for other types of articles.

Testimony from experts is a vital part of the feature article. It lends greater authority to the article, and sometimes, when more than one point of view on a topic is expressed by experts, it heightens reader interest. When you use an expert's testimony, give his or her full name (make sure you have written permission in advance to do so), as well as title and affiliation. In the article on single parenting, the free-lance writer used testimony from an expert in this way:

> Dr. Cora Scott, licensed clinical psychologist at Newburyport's Life Skills Unlimited . . . sees it as a healthy sign that more people are aware of the needs of greater psychological understanding and growth, that they read self-help books and parenting guides, and seek out professional help when necessary. In her words, "Even if the divorce rate

continues to go up and more people become single parents, individuals will strive to become more aware and earnestly attempt to grow and cope."

Many features include sidebars (with tips, facts, names and addresses of relevant organizations, information on related topics, or specific advice to the reader who may wish to pursue the topic on his or her own). The writer of the single-parenting article included a sidebar on "15 Do's for Single Parents," tips on how to cope with the situation and reduce the stress it has engendered.

Queries for feature articles

Read several issues of the publications that interest you and as many of the different types of articles in them as you can. Take note of the range of topics, writing styles, points of view, and approaches in these articles. Plan to build your feature article on this foundation, putting into practice the techniques you've learned for constructing various kinds of articles.

Your query for a feature must be thorough and well thought out, detailing the types of research you will do, the names of the experts you plan to contact (and whether you personally know them), and ideas for sidebars, where appropriate. If you have suggestions for effective illustrations—photos or graphs—include these, too, especially if you can provide them yourself. But major publications usually use their own professional illustrators and photographers.

Once you get the go-ahead for a feature, keep the editor aware of your progress on the article (if it is going to take more than a few weeks to complete). Because the feature is longer and more complex than other types of articles, you may have questions for the editor as you go along. Your research may suggest a different approach or point of view from the one you originally agreed upon, and you will want editorial approval before you make any such change. When you call or write the editor, ask whatever questions you feel are necessary, but make them specific and to the point, and try to cover as many as possible in a single phone call or letter.

Writing a publishable feature article is surely a goal for the free-lance writer, and best of all, it's an attainable goal. Don't be daunted by the idea of writing a full-length feature article. It requires the same skills that other types of articles demand. When you get your first go-ahead for a feature, approach it just as you would any other article: with professional work habits and attitude.

SPECIAL FIELDS

11

DEVELOPING A SPECIALTY

DEVELOPING A SPECIALTY IN ARTICLE WRITING is an extension of the old advice you've probably heard since you began to write: "Write what you know." Actually, however, it's advice that can and should be followed only to a limited degree. It would be better to say, "Write what you know or *can find out*." Specialty writing is more than writing about your vacation or your love of old furniture, although many specialties, like travel or antiques, often have their roots in personal experience. A writing specialty combines experience with knowledge and research and the skill to write about it persuasively, convincingly, and authoritatively.

Editors look to writers who are experts in various fields to give the material they publish credibility and authenticity. They want the most accurate, up-to-date information available on a subject, written in a readable, authoritative manner. For an article on where and how to go camping with children, a travel editor expects a writer to have experience in camping with children. Also, the writer must anticipate what the reader needs and wants to know, and be able to locate and present that information in a professionally written feature. In giving the writer a go-ahead for a specialty article, the editor is trusting the writer's knowledge and experience; it is the writer's job to justify that trust by producing an accurate, readable piece.

Specialty writers have to be more than just acquainted with their subjects. They must know where to go for research, whom to contact to unearth new and little-known information and check facts on the latest developments in the field. In addition, they must be able not only to write clearly about their subjects for readers who are not as familiar with the topic, but to write with a mixture of affection and expertise that makes the reader want to take up fly-fishing, plant a wildflower garden, start a recycling center, or volunteer at a hospital, to name a few specialty areas.

Having a specialty or expertise gives new writers an edge in several ways. It provides them with a subject area to focus on, it establishes their credibility, and it identifies markets.

Focus in a writer's career is just as important as focus in an article itself. Concentrating on a specific subject area helps the writer develop skills and knowledge in greater depth than would otherwise be possible. A writer with a specialty can write with greater authority about a subject than a person who dabbles in a variety of subjects, although many article writers write equally well and successfully on related topics or from a variety of angles.

Your specialty identifies you to an editor and establishes your credentials in a field. It also tells the editor that you are a professional. If the editor is aware that you have an area of expertise but doesn't want you to write the specific piece you have proposed, he or she may suggest another article related to your specialty, but with a different approach. For example, you might query the editor of a gardening magazine with an idea for an article on how to increase the yield from your small tomato patch. The editor may tell you that the magazine published a piece on that subject recently and suggest that you write a piece instead on containment or raised garden beds—how to build them and what grows best in them.

Sometimes a specialty takes on a life of its own. Once editors know that you are an expert in a particular field, they will tend to come to you for articles on that subject. And your knowledge of your specialty will increase and expand as you write about it successfully from different angles.

Cultivating a Specialty

You don't have to decide on a specialty before you begin to write articles, the way you had to declare a major in college. Most often, a writer's specialty evolves over a period of time, with writing experience. To get started, look in your own backyard. Literally. You may have an unusual garden. Or perhaps you've designed and built a jungle gym. Maybe you don't even have to go as far as your backyard. Do you collect baseball cards, antique costumes, or old phonograph records? What do you care most about? One free-lance writer who specializes in writing about outdoor recreation says, "The best writing reflects the things that you feel passionately about. I really enjoy the feeling of conveying to the reader what it's like to be in the outdoors." Another writer says that developing a specialty is "finding a need and having the experience that matches the need." Both of these writers are correct.

What are your hobbies? Are you skilled in handicrafts or woodworking? Do you build furniture? Have you renovated or redecorated your own house or apartment? Are you good at organizing committees or events in your town? Do you volunteer at your child's school? Are you an avid runner, walker, fly fisherman, bicyclist, sailor, windsurfer, skier, kayaker, golfer, bowler? Chances are, years of experience in any of these activities have given you more expertise than you realize. Read magazines and newspapers that specialize in those areas. Then think about what readers might need and want to know about the subject—that you can tell them in an intriguing and authoritative way.

Consider also your regular job. Are you an accountant, landscaper, paralegal, paramedic, electrician, salesperson, teacher, caterer, social worker, chemist, lawyer, computer programmer, musician, mechanic, or day-care provider? Your job requires experience and know-how that you can use as the springboard for an article. Or consider the jobs, professions, or occupations of your family, friends, and neighbors. You have probably absorbed more knowledge than you realize from conversation. From my husband, an environmental scientist, I have learned a great deal about the issues that face our surrounding communities as they try to cope with water scarcity and pollution, as well as sewage, construction, and conservation problems. Thus, in writing the article on the local wildlife refuge, I knew what questions to ask the director and how to present the answers clearly.

What is your educational background? Which subjects interested you most in school? If you went to college or graduate school, what did you major in? You don't need a graduate degree in a subject to write about it, but a strong interest or academic background, whether it's in business, science, history, or literature, gives you a foundation to build on, enhanced by reading and research about recent developments in these fields.

Sometimes, simply in the course of general free-lance writing, a writer finds a specialty developing. One now successful travel writer first approached the *Yankee Magazine* travel guide, offering to provide the editors with some information on Boston. Now, fifteen years later, he receives assignments to travel to the Caribbean, Europe, and Canada to research feature articles for such publications as *National Geographic Traveler*.

Tips on specialty writing

As a specialist, you are expected to know more than just the basics about a field and to keep up-to-date with the latest developments; but you're not expected to know everything. Instead, you need to know whom to call and where to go for the answers to readers' questions. Even when you present yourself as a specialist to an editor and to your readers, *never* pretend to know more than you do, and never guess at information or facts. You can be *sure* that some reader will catch your error! Making errors and not checking facts will definitely harm your reputation, and it may even harm a reader. For example, if you are writing about the risks of engaging in sports activities in hot weather, you need to know the difference between heat exhaustion and heat stroke, which is more dangerous, how to treat each safely, and when to get medical help.

Although your article should have a strong point of view, don't use your specialty as a pulpit or a soapbox, unless you are writing an op-ed piece. Save your emotions for opinion or personal experience columns. Although your specialty is something that obviously you care deeply about, your job as a writer is to present solid, accurate information that supports a point of view with some objectivity.

Different writing specialties require different skills and different types of research in addition to basic article writing skills. If you write about health and food, you need to know the fundamentals of good nutrition as well as what type of articles and information editors of health and food magazines, or general publications that use such material require. (You'll learn this by reading several issues of the publications that interest you.) Here's a sampling of health and nutrition article titles from the magazine *Eating Well*:

"Something Fishy at the Seafood Counter" (about the fresh seafood business)

"Rx for Recipes" (healthful approaches to family recipes)

"An Onion a Day" (remedies made from onions)

Find out in advance whether the readership of the publication you are aiming for knows more or less about your topic than you do. Is it geared to specialists or to general readers? If you are writing for a general publication, assume that your readers are intelligent but do not know about your subject in depth. In that case, define terms related to your field, even if they are familiar to you; define *tack cloth,* for instance, if you are writing about furniture refinishing. Identify and describe in correct sequence the basic steps in a process, even if as an expert you have done them so many times that they are second nature to you (how to make a clean cut with a hack saw, for example). On the other hand, don't patronize or talk down to the reader. Nothing loses a reader's interest more quickly.

When writing for a specialty publication, you can assume that your audience knows more than the general reader about your topic, so if your article is written at too basic a level, it will only frustrate and bore your readers. For example, you probably don't have to define *quadriceps* or *shin splints* for the readers of a fitness magazine, but it might be a good idea to refresh their memory on *glycogen*. If it's your first time writing for a particular publication, discuss the use of such terms or phrases with the editor after you are given a go-ahead.

Always be sure to use the correct terminology for your special field, but avoid jargon. If several different terms are commonly used for the same thing, use the one that best suits your audience and the publication. In writing about a system of health care for a health-care magazine, you can probably use the abbreviation *HMO;* but for a general newspaper, you'll want to use the term *health maintenance organization* the first time, then *HMO*.

Developing a specialty is an ongoing learning experience. Never think that you have learned everything there is to know about a subject. Fields change and develop; products become obsolete. Keep current in your field, with personalities, new techniques, products, discoveries and innovations. If you don't have a specialty now, you can develop one over a period of time. You may start with one field of interest and move on to another. As a writer, you have a head start: You are already curious about the world around you.

12

TRAVEL AND RECREATION

PICTURE YOURSELF HURTLING DOWN the Colorado River with fourteen other people in a huge, undulating rubber raft, and getting paid for it. Or perhaps you'd rather dine on champagne and caviar, listening to the smooth clack-clacking of train wheels gliding over the tracks on the *Orient Express*. At the end of the trip, you'd merely submit your receipts to an editor, dash off a brilliant, sophisticated article, and settle in to wait for a huge check and your name in glossy print.

A few travel and recreation writers do get to race through the wilds or bask in luxury—all expenses paid. A few of the elite writing community receive regular assignments from national magazines. But these people represent only a small proportion of travel and recreation writers. The travel and recreation writing field covers where people go and what they do in new and different places (or where they'd like to go and what they'd like to do there). Sure, occasionally this means far-flung trips and adventures. But more often—for writers and for readers—this means a weekend getaway to a nearby inn or a day trip to a state park. And that's the beauty of travel and recreation writing: You can begin learning how to write travel pieces in your own backyard.

Travel and recreation are intertwined: People travel to places for recreation, education, and just for pleasure, whether it's paddling a canoe, visiting Disney World, or strolling through the San Diego Zoo or the Museum of Modern Art in New York. So the travel writer usually also writes about recreation, and recreation articles often appear in the travel sections of magazines and newspapers, and throughout general magazines, food magazines, and inflight magazines.

Because of the diversity of people's interests and the wide range of publications that publish travel and recreation articles, the topics are just about endless. A travel or recreation article can focus on the vacation as a whole or a specific aspect or site of a trip: how to buy handmade rugs in Kathmandu or how to pack a backpack for a hut-to-hut ski trip in Norway. I know a travel writer who wrote an article on how to transport a canoe by train. (Such short, specific stories are often expanded into longer features for later publication.)

Subjects for travel and recreation articles can focus on any of the following:

Full-scale vacations, both domestic and overseas. These range from luxurious resorts to adventure travel, from organized tours to spontaneous getaways. Article topics might include how to tour Ireland on a budget; locations of the best beaches in Florida; how to order dinner in a restaurant in India; and which are the best campgrounds in Yellowstone National Park.

Trips planned around hobbies or special interests. History or military buffs visit battlegrounds of the Civil War; golf enthusiasts flock to St. Andrews in Scotland every year; railroad enthusiasts take planned or casual trips by rail. An article might cover finding the best out-of-the-way antique shops in Vermont; visiting a dude ranch in Colorado; touring famous gardens of Natchez, Mississippi (or any other notable garden here or abroad); and exploring the wine country of northern California.

Trips planned around special events and holidays. People travel to places to attend special events, such as Mardi Gras, the Super Bowl, Shakespeare festivals, the Santa Fe Opera, and the famous Paleo horse race in Siena. If you live in an area that hosts a special event, you can write, for instance, about good vantage spots for viewing the Boston Marathon; sights to see while visitors are in your town for a convention; and taking the Christmas Stroll on Nantucket.

Trips that appeal to families. Planning an unusual vacation that will appeal to both adults and children is a constant quest for many families. A good travel article can steer families toward that ideal vacation, with such topics as the best aquariums or children's museums in New England; touring the Baseball Hall of Fame in Cooperstown, NY; how to travel through Europe with a young child; and how to find a restaurant or inn that caters to families.

Romantic getaways. Everyone dreams of a romantic getaway from time to time, whether it's a weekend at a country inn or a week in Bermuda. Travel articles that focus on romantic getaways usually emphasize physical beauty, easy access, relaxation, leisure, and privacy. Possible topics: visiting the coastal village of Mendocino in northern California; a list of Chicago hotels that offer weekend getaway packages; the best spots for secluded picnics along the coast of Maine; how to choose an ocean cruise; and a list of country inns that *don't* cater to families.

Short getaways. Day trips and weekend getaways are as popular as longer vacations. You can write an article about them with very little travel and expense. It's a great way to get started in travel and recreation writing, with articles on two or three little-known but beautiful state parks; village museums such as Sturbridge, Massachusetts, or Canterbury, New Hampshire; whale watching; good spots for kite flying; or day cruises from city harbors such as New York or San Francisco.

As you think about a topic for your article, ask yourself if you would enjoy the trip or activity; if not, don't write about it. Enthusiasm is important in travel and recreation writing. Finally, focus your topic idea and do appropriate research to enable you to give readers complete, specific information, not just sketchy, superficial impressions.

Travel and recreation articles should give readers all the information they need to embark on a trip or activity; for example, advice on what to do if you arrive in a strange or foreign city without a hotel reservation, or if you lose your passport, luggage, tickets, or money. Some travel articles recount personal experiences with accompanying sidebars that provide necessary information for a similar trip. For example, a personal experience piece on boating on the Danube might include a sidebar listing travel agencies, rates, packing tips, and the best months for this type of trip. As you work on yours, keep in mind the following tips:

If possible, visit the location you are writing about. Record both facts and your personal impressions about the place and your experience there. Much information can be found in almanacs, guidebooks, through chambers of commerce, public relations departments of hotels, and in libraries.

In writing about seasonal topics, remember that magazines work far in advance of publication, so if you want to write about spring garden tours, you'll have to query the publication six months to a year in advance of the time the article would be published. The major magazines like *Travel & Leisure, Conde Nast Traveler,* and women's magazines have even longer lead times.

Offer photographs if you are a proficient photographer (you don't have to be a professional). The editor can always decide to use stock photos or professional photographs instead, but will appreciate your offer.

A sidebar can provide travel directions, items to pack, and relevant names and addresses.

Your article should include the following:

1. A brief description and/or definition of special events or activities occurring in the place itself (including specific travel directions as well as methods of travel, if appropriate).

2. A list of any items the traveler needs to take—specialized gear or clothing, or items that simply make the trip more comfortable.

3. Important addresses and phone numbers of places to stay, restaurants, important resources (such as consulates, travel agencies, or park services) that readers may want to contact. These *must* be accurate and up-to-date. Call or write to each one to confirm all information.

4. Prices and fees: admission fees to museums, the average prices of meals at restaurants (grouping these by

inexpensive, moderate, and expensive is helpful). These must be accurate and current as well. Readers should be cautioned that these are subject to change.

5. Information on climate and weather. Give the facts about seasonal changes for states like Minnesota, with its wide ranges of temperature, rainfall, snow, and heat.

6. A list of required documentation, passports, visas, proof of immunization.

7. Tips for safe and fun travel. Give the reader an idea of what to expect from the experience. You might offer advice on how to negotiate the maze of parking facilities or escalators in a particular airport, like O'Hare in Chicago; or remind readers to wear a helmet and bright clothing when bicycling. If the country or region you are writing about has customs different from those of the U.S., advise readers of important points that will help them to avoid embarrassment. When readers finish your article, they should be ready to enjoy the trip or experience.

If you are writing a personal experience travel and recreation article, your own experiences should convey both information and enthusiasm. Give an account of the trip you've taken, whether it's a day at the county fair or a two-week trek through the mountains of New Zealand. Use details that appeal to the senses, so readers can see the soft pastels of the desert, hear the coyotes howl, smell the rain coming, taste the strong coffee, and feel grains of sand between their toes. Your personal experience article, like a good short story, should create tension and drama. It should have a climax—the summit of the mountain or the dive down the tracks of a 100-foot-high roller coaster, or the mule trip into the Grand Canyon, or the flight in a small plane at sunrise over Ayer's Rock in

Australia. And a sidebar can provide facts that prepare readers to take the trip themselves.

Where to sell travel articles

There is a large range of markets for travel and recreation articles, from the obvious—inflight magazines and *Travel & Leisure*—to the not-so-obvious general magazines, local newspapers, and magazines such as *Early American Life*. Women's magazines, such as *Glamour* and *Modern Bride,* often have travel sections. Regional magazines, such as *Yankee* and *New Jersey Monthly,* feature travel and recreation opportunities within their geographic area. Specialized travel and recreation magazines, such as *Gourmet, Outside, Tours & Resorts,* and *RV Times Magazine,* focus on specific types of travel and activities that appeal to their readers. Newspapers, both big-city and community or regional, publish travel and recreation stories. Finally, don't overlook the "small" departments of larger publications—the departments that publish 100-word items on travel and recreation. If you sell a few such pieces, eventually you may build up your credits and have a foot in the door for future sales.

As you develop an idea for a travel and recreation article, study the publications that you think would be most appropriate for your piece. Consider who the readers are, what their interests are, and what type of activity is most likely to appeal or be available to them. Finally, check the masthead of the publication to see if there is a travel editor, and send your query directly to that person (or call the publication to find out the name of the articles or travel editor). Always address your queries or manuscript to a person by name. *People* answer letters; magazines do not.

Travel and recreation writing is an exciting specialty, but it's not without its difficulties. Sometimes writers take trips only to realize there just isn't enough material for an article, or the editor decides to cancel the story. After getting the go-ahead from an editor, I once climbed Mt. Washington in northern New Hampshire in winter—thirteen hours trudging through snow, with winds gusting to 118 miles per hour—only to have the editor later change his mind about the type of article he wanted. But this one experience didn't stop me from writing subsequent travel and recreation articles.

13

SPORTS AND FITNESS

YOU DON'T HAVE TO BE A TRIATHLETE or body builder to write about sports and fitness, but it helps to have experience in and enthusiasm for physical activity. If you walk to work each morning, attend aerobics classes several times a week, ride your bicycle on weekends, go fishing in a local pond, or play a round of golf occasionally, you are already involved in sports and fitness activities. As a free-lance writer, you can parlay these interests into published articles.

In today's sports- and fitness-conscious society, topics for articles abound. Peruse a few magazines and newspapers and you'll see that they regularly publish articles on topics ranging from salmon fishing in Alaska to safe exercise during pregnancy. Subjects for sports and fitness articles generally fall into three broad categories:

Events. Many sports and fitness articles (both in magazines and newspapers) center on an actual event, whether it's a basketball game, a walk-a-thon, a tennis match, or a bicycle race. These articles report on the details of the event, the participants, and the outcome. Of course, timing is crucial for approaching a publication to ask for a go-ahead to cover a sporting event; and it really must be 1) important enough to have wide appeal, and 2) one that would not be covered by a regular reporter or sports columnist. You must contact the editor well ahead of the event.

Participation. Whether it's rock climbing, mountain biking, horseback riding, camping, sailing, rowing, deep-sea fishing, tennis, croquet, or billiards, every sport has a number of angles from which to approach it in writing. Don't just think of your sport as a whole; break it down into parts: training, outdoor conditions, equipment, techniques, clothing, food, and where to go. How to dress properly for running in cold weather; assessing weather conditions during a mountain hike; the best "hidden" fishing spots in your region; how to use the gears on a 10-speed bike for maximum efficiency; and suggestions for easy warm-up and cool-down exercises for people who are just getting into shape—all are appropriate subjects for articles in this field. In addition, some sports, such as sea kayaking, have an ancient and fascinating history; others, like jet skiing, are brand new. Thus, you might write about different aspects of the sport or the new groups of people—elderly or handicapped—participating in it.

Think about a new angle on a popular or old subject. Everyone has read about athletes who take steroids or amphetamines. But what about athletes and alcohol? There are successful and talented athletes who are also alcoholics. How does this affect their performance, their health, and their families?

Many families participate in sports and fitness activities together, so articles aimed at them are helpful and popular. Consider doing a feature on gyms or health clubs that cater to families; campgrounds designed for families; how to choose the right backpack (or skis, bicycle, etc.) for a child; or how to introduce a child to a particular sport.

Profiles. Many sports and fitness articles are profiles of the people who participate in specific activities. While you might not have a chance to interview a famous quarterback or pitcher, you might get an even more interesting interview with a rock climber who is paralyzed from the waist down, or the oldest person to climb Mt. Whitney, in California. Perhaps you'll have an opportunity to interview a participant in the Special Olympics or the wheelchair competition of the Boston Marathon. Or consider the people who are on the sidelines: for instance, the families of professional triathletes. How do these families help support the athlete? Does the whole family change its diet to meet the needs of the triathlete? Does anyone in the family run, bike, or swim with the athlete to keep him or her company? Does anyone in the family sacrifice his or her own interests, adjust schedules and mealtimes to meet those of the athlete? These questions are just the seeds of an article you might develop. Note also that these questions apply to any serious athlete, whether amateur or professional—even those who are in elementary and high school.

Related subjects

Keep in mind the relationship between sports and fitness and other aspects of life. For example, insurance for athletes and nutrition for high-altitude climbing illustrate connections to business and health.

Sports and fitness articles convey facts as well as enthusiasm for the activities they focus on. As you develop your idea for a sports or fitness article, keep in mind the following:

1. Become familiar with editors' interests in particular fields of sports and fitness by analyzing several issues of the magazines for which you want to write your articles. A writer who specializes in articles on skiing notes, "In the outdoor market, themes are more important than events. These magazines get a million queries about a race, a climb, or an expedition. But themes—such as how expeditions struggle for funding—are much better. . . . A theme is timeless." There is a larger window in which to run a story on a theme than for an event.

2. Keep current on developments and achievements in the sports and fitness field, but don't rely on TV reports or rumors for your research. Conduct a thorough investigation of events and trends by consulting with experts and reading the sports sections of newspapers and the specialty publications for which you hope to write.

3. Use correct terminology, but avoid jargon. Terminology will often depend on the magazine—specialized publications will use more technical terms than general publications. If your article gives instructions on how to improve in tennis, be sure to define and describe clearly each of the different strokes and its function in the game.

4. In your query to the editor, suggest possible illustrations for your article, and supply rough sketches if possible. A how-to article on recommended and safe stretching exercises during early pregnancy will be greatly

improved by line drawings or photographs depicting a woman doing the exercises. If you can supply photographs, offer them to the editor.

Where to submit your articles

Markets for sports and fitness articles range from highly specialized and technical magazines to local newspapers. The focus of a magazine is obvious in its title: *American Fitness, Canoe, Tennis, Bird Watcher's Digest, National Racquetball, Salt Water Sportsman, Woman Bowler,* and *Golf Digest.* Others, such as *Chesapeake Bay Magazine* and *Harrowsmith,* though not immediately perceived as markets, do buy sports and fitness articles. Many general magazines and newspapers have sports and fitness departments that buy short pieces from free lancers, and regional magazines like *California Horse Review* and *Lakeland Boating* focus on sports and sporting events in a particular geographical area.

Study market listings as well as general and specialized magazines to see what type of sports and fitness articles they publish. Note whether the magazine publishes personal experience articles on sports or only how-to, where-to articles. Are readers apt to be experts at the sport or newcomers? Do they have a general interest or one that is more specialized and technical? For example, *Bicycling* reaches a wider audience than *Mountain Bike.* If you are querying a newspaper and aren't certain which department to try, read through the sports, travel and lifestyle sections to determine where sports and fitness articles by free lancers appear. Find the name of the appropriate editor in the paper, or phone to ask before writing.

Don't be afraid to enter the world of writing about sports if you aren't a World Cup athlete. If sports and fitness interest you, your enthusiasm for the subject and your knowledge of article writing will make for a winning combination.

14

HEALTH

HEALTH IS A NATIONAL PREOCCUPATION. From such issues as nutrition and diet, illness and well being, even birth and death, to issues related to health care, health insurance and hospitals, we deal with our own health and the health of others every day. Thus, the opportunities for free-lance articles are legion.

Topics for health articles abound. If you focus and research your idea thoroughly, the chances are good that you will find a home for your article. Although subject areas certainly overlap and not *every* topic falls into a particular category, it's helpful to think of health topics in one of the following ways.

General Health. This includes both physical and mental health. Article topics might include the controversies surrounding drugs such as RU486, Ritalin, and Prozac; the nutritional value of school breakfasts and lunches; drug abuse by doctors; how to buy safe toys for toddlers; how people cope with such chronic illnesses as multiple sclerosis, muscular dystrophy and Alzheimer's; how parents respond when they learn a son or daughter is homosexual; how a surviving spouse copes with the suicide of a husband or wife; how to tell a child about death; health problems of the homeless; an examination of "anti-aging" cosmetics and other products; a comparison of prices and ingredients and effectiveness of generic and brand-name medications and health products; the effect of "secondary smoke" on nonsmokers in the work or social setting, and at home on the family, especially children; how to deal with a smoker who insists on "lighting up" in a group in which the nonsmokers object—or actually get sick from smoke.

Health care. This is a very broad topic and includes the business side of health care and the professional health care workers, providers, administrators, planners, and insurers. You may consider writing about such specifics as the publicly supported hospital that has to try to survive continual budget cuts and the effect its closing would have on the community; the fact that millions of people in the country have no health insurance coverage at all, and millions more have inadequate coverage; what happens to patients who are discharged from the hospital too soon and have no one to care for them at home. Another topic could deal with a profile of an emergency-room nurse or doctor who has to make life-and-death decisions every day and the emotional effect on that person.

The possibilities seem endless and can further cover the evaluation of health maintenance organizations versus traditional health insurance coverage—advantages and disadvantages of each system; how to choose a nursing home for an elderly relative and what the alternatives are; where chronically ill patients, young or old, can obtain long-term care, as in the case of a young adult person who has cerebral palsy and needs residential care and educational opportunities; alternative or holistic treatment for patients suffering from cancer or other progressive diseases (multiple sclerosis, muscular dystrophy); the hospice movement; pros and cons of using a midwife or a physician for childbirth; profiles of some little known but important health researchers; and health-care scams, from diet programs to programs that promise eternal youth or miraculous treatment for a terminal disease, and medications that make unsupported or false health claims.

Other ideas for health articles may be found in daily newspapers, magazines, health newsletters, and other publications in which health features appear regularly. Observe the health care problems and issues that pervade your own life and those of your neighbors, friends, and relatives.

Writing an article for the health market requires the same skills that other fields demand, plus a few specific extras that you can learn as you go more deeply into the subject. Here are some special guidelines to keep in mind when writing health articles:

1. Do your research thoroughly. Interview experts whenever possible. In addition to regular sources of information, hunt down the nearest medical library (call a nearby hospital and ask if there is one in the vicinity that a layperson can use), and familiarize yourself with terms and trends. Peruse publications such as *The New England Journal of Medicine* and *The Journal of the American Medical Association* (usually available in large public libraries or special libraries) to learn what is happening in the field and to get ideas for articles. Many hospitals, such as Massachusetts General Hospital in Boston, also publish newsletters that are available to the

public. Before you query an editor in the health field, do enough research so that you can write an authoritative, knowledgeable query on the subject.

2. Keep up to date, not only with trends, but with changing public and professional attitudes. Topics that were until relatively recently taboo or unknown and unexplored—premenstrual syndrome, homosexuality (controversial at the past several psychiatric national conferences, for instance), could very well be in the mainstream of health writing today. Another recent advance has to do with a national health program, until quite recently strongly opposed by the American Medical Association, and now widely written about and discussed by doctors across the country. Many doctors are now changing their views and attitudes on the subject. You might do a round-up article on the opinions of doctors, nurses, hospital administrators, average citizens, union members, ministers, and citizens in various economic and social levels on the subject of a national health program and how they feel about it.

New discoveries in medicine and medical technology, as well as biogenetics, are widely discussed in newspapers, and the ways in which these breakthrough developments can be used for the benefit of people will make lively reading, especially if you quote a few "experts" as well as the general public.

3. Most important in writing health articles is to relate what you write about to the experience of people and the effects of your subject on them. Because the health and health care field tends to deal with technical and complex issues, it's especially important to remember this rule of thumb as you develop your article. For example, an article on the effects of air pollution on the human

body captures reader attention only when the writer illustrates the point with specific cases, perhaps those who suffer from respiratory diseases and live in urban areas, or friends, relatives, or neighbors.

4. Use correct terminology, but try to keep your article lively, easy to read, and free of medical jargon. Emphasize how your health article will or could have a positive effect on the readers or their families.

Marketing your health articles

Markets for articles in the health field are wide ranging, from general to highly specialized publications. Local newspapers, regional magazines, and women's and national magazines as well as health magazines with narrowly defined audiences all publish health articles. Actually a very large majority of *all* publications—magazines and newspapers, general and specialized—regularly publish articles on some aspect of health and well being.

Before querying a publication, study it not only for content but for editorial scope and focus. This will help you avoid the mistake of querying a magazine on vegetarian nutrition with an idea for an article on the nutritional qualities of the new lower fat fast-food hamburgers.

Some of the publications that focus specifically on the health-care field include *American Journal of Nursing, American Medical News,* and *The Physician and Sportsmedicine. American Baby, Working Mother,* and *New Woman* all publish articles on health as it relates to women and children. *Eating Well* deals with healthful eating. Magazines such as *Recovery Life* look for inspirational, personal experience articles on recovery from a serious illness. You will find browsing in the library or on a large newsstand one of the most productive uses of your time. Not only will it help you think about health from countless perspectives that might not previously have occurred to you, but it will provide you with ideas and subjects for which there is a market.

You can enter the field of writing about health from personal experience that is reinforced by research. The field is wide open, and of vital interest to everyone, witnessed by the fact that just about every style of magazine and newspaper uses health-related articles. You may find yourself a new specialty that is always unfolding with new discoveries, new challenges, and new article writing opportunities.

15

Hobbies, Crafts, and Collectibles

COMPLEX LIVES, TIGHTER BUDGETS, and taking pleasure in creativity and a job well done have merged to produce a thriving culture of hobbyists, craftspeople, and collectors. Life in the fast lane has made people relish their leisure, even if it's only a few minutes a day or a few hours each weekend. Limited time and resources for travel have increased interest in activities that can be pursued at home or within a short range of home, and part of that participation involves reading about these activities in magazines and newspapers. Where there are readers, there is a need for free-lance writers to produce articles that instruct and inform readers about the homemade and handmade, from photography to folk art painting to the collecting of unique objects in specific fields of interest.

Hobbies

Hobbies run the gamut from cooking to photography to raising tropical fish to operating ham radios—and consequently, the range of opportunities for writing about hobbies is tremendous. This chapter will comment briefly on hobbies in general and then concentrate on two major areas for free-lance writers who are interested in writing about hobbies: crafts and collectibles.

Of course it's best to become as knowledgeable about a hobby as possible by engaging in it yourself—whether it's birdwatching, flower arranging, cooking Mexican food, building model airplanes, or doing crossword puzzles. Dive into a hobby that you expect to enjoy as much as the diehard enthusiasts do. In addition, read the specialty publications associated with the hobby—*Finescale Modeler, The Autograph Collector's Magazine,* or *Games*—to get ideas for articles. Attend related events, conventions, and meetings; talk with people immersed in the activity. Through research and participation, you can become proficient enough in a hobby to write about it. Don't write about a hobby if you aren't interested in it. Your lack of enthusiasm will show in your writing.

Crafts

Editors of crafts magazines are always looking for new ideas for articles that generally center on two areas: ideas and instructions for original projects; and how-to techniques for creating a wide range of items or for solving technical craft problems.

Original projects can range from needlework to woodwork, but the key word is *original;* the idea must be entirely yours, not an adaptation of someone else's. Keep in mind that previously published craft designs are protected by copyright law, and you may not use any part of such designs in a project you intend to publish. This doesn't mean that the technique (brush stroke or stitch) must be new, but the project itself must be new.

"A salable idea [for a craft project] is one that's fairly easy to make, isn't too time-consuming, and is different from anything else that's been published," advises a crafts writer. But she goes on to caution writers that articles on projects that are *too* unusual are not likely to sell. Most editors like crafts projects that are functional as well as decorative.

Simplified techniques for working on a craft project and new solutions to craft problems are also welcome at crafts magazines. For example, you might have an idea for a new way to keep your fabric clean while working on it, as with cross-stitching; or for mixing household products that work as well as more expensive commercial products, perhaps for sealing wood before decorating it with folk art.

The vast majority of crafts articles are how-to pieces that give clear, step-by-step instructions for creating a project or solving a problem. Obviously, to write for the crafts market it helps if you are a craftsperson yourself. Never try to develop ideas for crafts articles if you haven't worked through the projects or techniques yourself and have a high level of proficiency. In addition, keep in mind the following:

1. Even if the magazine uses its own photographer for the finished article, you must send color prints of the finished project with your query. This means that you must complete the project before querying the magazine, but that's a good idea in any case, since it gives you a chance to work out the kinks and make sure your instructions are complete and concise. A 35-mm camera is

best. Although not every magazine requires you to send more than one picture, it's best to include two or three—one of the completed project by itself, and perhaps one of the item as it will be used (on the Christmas tree, in a table setting). Don't mail the completed item with your query. This is the mark of an amateur, and more important, you may never have your work returned.

2. Since magazines want specific instructions for each step of the crafting process, make a list of materials, diagrams and patterns, measurements, and stitching or brush stroke instructions as you work on the project. Your directions will flow more smoothly if you have these lists to work from.

3. Your crafts article should first describe the project or item—what it is and what it's used for—then list materials needed. Next, take the reader through each step of the how-to process, making sure to point out ways to handle tricky problems.

4. When you are ready to write down your instructions—in addition to the information you've compiled above—be sure to include any special hints, references to figures (drawings, graphs, etc.), information on size (in clothing), knitting gauge, and necessary abbreviation of terms. (Learn the correct terms and abbreviations used in your craft. For example, in knitting instructions, "yo" means "yarn over" and "k" means "knit.") If possible, after you write your directions, ask another experienced crafter who is not familiar with your particular project (but is knowledgeable in the general area) to read them to see that they are clear. Rewrite any step that the reader had trouble with.

5. When you've completed the project, examine it closely and objectively to be certain that it is of profes-

sional quality. Would you buy it if you saw it in a crafts shop? Don't try to hide flaws; the magazine depends on high-quality photographs and projects to present to readers. If it isn't perfect, keep the flawed item for yourself and rework the project for the magazine.

6. When the editor gives you a go-ahead for the article and requests the actual project, package it carefully so that it will arrive undamaged. If a picture of the project is going to appear in a magazine, the item must arrive as fresh as it was when you completed it. (The project will be returned to you after publication.)

Markets

Aside from general women's magazines and newspapers (which sometimes publish profiles of craftspeople), crafts publications are quite specialized. The crafts market has fairly strict guidelines, but they are easy to follow, and this market offers opportunities for beginners and experienced free-lance writers alike.

Crafts magazines are aimed specifically at readers who use the magazines to improve their skills, make new projects, and get ideas. But each of these magazines has a different focus and audience. *McCall's Needlework & Crafts* is aimed at readers who are interested in a variety of projects—some of which can be completed in an evening, and others that are more complex and take longer to complete. But the emphasis is on quality of design. *Crafts 'n' Things* also deals with various crafts, but concentrates on the quick and easy-to-make designs, encouraging new crafters as well as new crafts designers. In all cases, accuracy and clarity are essential.

Writing for guidelines even before querying is an absolute must in the crafts market. Each magazine has specific requirements, some very detailed, as well as strict deadlines. (This results in part from the scheduling of issues devoted to specific holiday projects, such as Christmas, Thanksgiving, and Valentine's Day.) Some crafts magazines concentrate on a single craft, like needlework or painting. You should be certain of the level of difficulty of the projects in a magazine before querying. Following all the guidelines will save you and the editor frustration and confusion.

COLLECTIBLES

To write about collectibles, you need to be a good reporter. You want to be not just in step with trends in collecting, but a step ahead whenever possible. No one can make foolproof predictions about collecting trends, which change constantly, but the observant writer can detect those that are unusual or likely to become popular. One successful writer for this market predicts that folk art and Victoriana will continue to generate strong interest in the coming years. Part of the fun of collecting is the gamble that today's collectibles (such as baseball cards and comic books) will increase in popularity and value. And the collectibles writer trots right along with collectors, enjoying the sometimes bumpy ride.

If you are a collector yourself or are interested in writing about antiques and collectibles, read antiques newspapers, auction reports, and magazines (as well as daily or weekly newspapers) to stay alert for trends. Be on the lookout for the unusual; the antiques newspaper *Mass Bay Antiques* ran a story about a man who collects cereal boxes! Talk to relatives and friends about their collections. Scour your own house for collectible ideas. Do you still have that collection of stuffed animals or Matchbox cars from your childhood? What about old books? Autographs? Antique postcards, photographs, even period clothing like Victorian hats and costume jewelry are collectibles.

An article for the collectibles market might report on an estate sale of rare books; describe how to authenticate a piece of period furniture; explain where to buy Zapotec weavings or Tibetan rugs. Sometimes a collector is as unusual as a collection itself and could lead you to writing an intriguing profile. A trip to the collector's home, an interview in his or her surroundings, as well as glimpses of the collection, can combine to create an article that is colorful and informative. Or you might decide to research the history of banjo timepieces or hunt down the truth about a hoax, a mysterious theft, or an extravagant deal.

The collectibles writer must share the collectors' enthusiasm for a particular area of interest. Collectors are passionate about what they collect, which may represent a slice of history or record the way things were twenty or two hundred years ago. Here are a few additional tips:

1. All articles on collectibles require research. A writer who specializes in this type of article comments, "Collectors are a bit obsessive, and they will read everything published about the item they collect. In order to be convincing, you have to know more than your readers do—that's not easy." So you need to learn as much as you can about your subject, from experts, collectors, critics, antiques and collectibles publications, and your own experiences at auctions or galleries. If possible, subscribe to a few of the antiques publications to keep abreast of trends and prices.

2. When describing or reporting on a collectible, iden-

tify its important characteristics, its condition, and where and when it was made. If you are reporting on the sale of a collection, include prices of the pieces sold, and be certain they are current and accurate. Collectors depend on this information to keep them apprised of trends in the market.

3. If you are writing a profile of a collector, you must do double research—on the collector as well as the collection—in order to ask intelligent questions and listen to the collector with understanding. An interview with an artist, in which you watch him or her at work and tour the home or studio, can also provide readers with as much information about the works of art as about the artist.

4. Publications vary on the question of photographs, so it's best to let the editor make the decision. If you can provide good-quality 35-mm photos, offer them to the editor (newspapers usually want black-and-white prints, magazines, color slides), but don't pretend to be a professional photographer if you aren't. Editors will see the difference quite quickly.

Markets

Collectibles publications vary widely, often overlapping with the antiques, hobby, and/or art markets. They range from the glossy monthly *Art & Antiques* to *Mass Bay Antiques,* a monthly antiques and collectibles newspaper centered on New England, or *Antiques & Auction News,* a weekly newspaper that buys articles on both collectors and their collections. More specialized publications such as *Teddy Bear Review* and *Sports Collectors Digest* focus on particular types of collections. Further, home decorating magazines often publish articles on collectibles because beyond the major elements of decorating (renovating and painting), collectibles can help make a room or home completely individual. (Also remember, furniture can fall into the category of collectibles, whether antique or not.) Certain collectibles are very affordable, and readers of a home decorating magazine may be encouraged to spruce up a room with collectibles rather than gutting the room and completely redecorating.

The arts and living sections of newspapers often feature stories about collectibles of individual collectors, as well as folk painters, potters, or woodcarvers who produce art objects that are considered collectible.

As you examine the publications you are considering querying, take special note of the level of detail and expertise you will be required to provide in an article. One writer who specializes in this area notes, "An article on Biedermeier furniture for *Magazine Antiques* should have a more scholarly tone and an intelligent, well-detailed description about the pieces . . . while an article for one of the regional newspapers might give a general description of a roll-top desk and concentrate more on how much money it's worth."

16

HOME AND GARDEN

WHETHER A COUNTRY FARMHOUSE OR CITY HIGHRISE, a home reflects lifestyle, taste, and values. A garden—in the form of a flower box clinging to the window of a tenth-floor apartment; a lush, half-acre vegetable garden filled with tomatoes, corn, pumpkins, peppers, and cucumbers; or plants potted in containers on a redwood deck—reflects the residents' personality and taste and gives individuality to a house.

Magazines that let readers fantasize and give them practical ideas for making their lifestyle dreams come true are most appealing to readers. There are home and garden magazines that cater to a wide range of lifestyles and tastes, from *Country Journal* to *Metropolitan Home*. Whether you want to build a backyard shed, plant a meadow of wildflowers, or build your own swimming pool, there is a magazine that can tell you how. The markets for free-lance articles in this field are abundant, as are the general or regional and city publications that regularly publish home and garden pieces.

There are so many possible topics for articles on home and garden—from remodeling kitchens to holiday entertaining to building rock gardens—that perhaps the toughest job for a writer is to come up with an unusual slant and focus for a publishable article idea. Look around you. Observe the problems you and your neighbors have in your own gardens or homes (remodeling, pest control) and how you solve them; work with (or watch) a friend on a building or renovating project; visit home furnishing departments and shows, as well as nurseries.

All types of articles, from service (how-to, where-to) to profiles and personal experience pieces find their way into home and garden publications.

What to write about

Around the home: When and how to clean house gutters safely and properly; how to remodel and renovate a room inexpensively; how to weatherstrip windows and doors for cold winters; how to wash a house covered in vinyl siding without scratching the finish; how to build bookshelves in an original and inexpensive way; a profile of a modern-day chimney sweep or of a carpenter who restores old barns; how to convert a garage into usable living space; how to build a New England-style dry wall; where to buy discount wall coverings; using unusual objects (patterned and colorful sheets or bedspreads for tablecloths or dish towels as placemats) to create a beautiful table setting; how to give a theme dinner or birthday party on a budget; and how to increase your closet space.

In the garden: A humorous, personal experience article on battling moles, raccoons, red squirrels, crows, Japanese beetles, gypsy moths, and other pests in the garden or under the porch; how to get evergreens to grow in clay-packed soil; a profile of a child who has an unusual garden; a list of the best garden supply or seed catalogues; where to buy rare plants that will grow in a particular region; a feature on indigenous plants and flowers that are endangered; how to use organic pest control or weed killer; how to build a garden bench; how to plant a garden in a small space; how to recognize plants that can cause allergies, are poisonous or unsafe (and shouldn't be planted where children or pets live)—like oleander, dieffenbachia, or belladonna.

Keep abreast of popular decorating styles and types of gardens in the home and garden market. One trend that has remained strong in magazine articles is "country" decorating, gardening, and furnishings. This style is covered by such magazines as *Country Home, Country Journal,* and *Country Living,* with articles on the country lifestyle that range from how to buy a secondhand tractor to how to find bargains at flea markets to how to convert a garage apartment to look like a country cottage.

In addition, gardening editors now seem to lean toward home landscaping and ornamental plants rather than vegetable gardens (although this certainly doesn't mean an editor won't be interested in a good, unusual idea for an article on vegetable gardens). They are also very much interested in pieces on environmental topics: pollution, recycling, waste disposal, water and energy conservation—but make it original.

Observe the world around you and read newspapers with an eye to finding good article topics in the home and garden field, and follow these tips to help you write publishable pieces:

1. Become familiar with your subject through research and talking to people whose homes you admire. If you

plan to write an article on different fabrics for window treatments, send to the fabric companies for information about their products. Or if you're planning an article on Holland tulip bulbs or herb gardens, write to the catalogue companies for more information. Don't make your article read like an advertisement for any of these companies; but use the information that describes the properties of various herbs and how to grow them to provide background for your piece, and make it authoritative.

2. When querying the home and garden magazines or home and garden sections of newspapers, consider the climate of the area that the publication (if it is local or regional) serves. Make sure that the project you intend to inform readers about (such as weatherstripping a house for cold weather) or the plant you are telling people how to care for is suited to that area's weather and seasons.

3. Know when to use technical terms, particularly in gardening articles. For instance, many gardening magazines include the Latin (botanical) names for plants, as well as the popular names, so when you write for one of these magazines, use the common name first, followed by the botanical name underlined and in parentheses—e.g., hollyhock *(Althea rosa)* or the mayflower bush *(Viburnum)*. The first word of the Latin name, which represents the *genus,* or family the plant belongs to, is capitalized. Newspapers and other general publications don't usually use the botanical terms for plants, but if you include them the editor can always remove them. (This is much easier than trying to add them later on.)

4. Supply photographs to accompany your articles, or offer them to the editor, unless you know that the magazine uses its own photographers. Your photos should be

taken with a 35-mm camera, either black-and-white prints or color slides, depending on the publication's specifications.

Articles on home and garden appear in many different types of publications. One gardening writer says, "Plants are inherently interesting to people, and garden articles can be slanted toward climate, beauty, travel, the environment, landscaping, hobbies, and even toward business—I once included a profile of a local nurseryman in a piece for *Small Business Opportunities*."

General interest, women's, family, decorating, gardening, and food magazines as well as lifestyle sections of newspapers are all markets for home and garden articles. Magazines such as *Farm and Ranch Living, Flower & Garden Magazine, Independent Living,* and *National Gardening Magazine* all publish articles by free-lance writers.

Several of the country magazines, such as *Country Home* and *Country Living,* have readers' forum columns with personal experience articles on country life. These columns can be a good place to get started in this market, and though you don't have to *live* in the country to write about it, you must have some personal experience with country life to make what you write convincing.

Like many other areas, the home and garden market is changing constantly. Thus, it is important for the writer to be observant and keep current with changing trends and attitudes, as well as new publications. (Look at the periodical sections in libraries and at large newsstands to keep abreast of the many new publications that emerge in this market, and their needs.) Also, study several issues of general mass market magazines, regional and inflight magazines, to see if they use home and/or garden pieces, or articles on famous gardens open to the public (some not well known outside the immediate area).

Writing for the home and garden market can provide an almost limitless range of opportunities for writers because of the rich diversity of publications. This market reaffirms one of the basic values of our society: No matter how cosmopolitan or complex it becomes, there's no place like home.

17

Money Matters

Money and business aren't confined to Wall Street. They are a pervasive part of the daily lives of all workers and consumers. Household budgeting, planning for retirement, purchasing a home or automobile, managing income, and choosing insurance are just a few examples of the areas of daily life that are affected by money.

All types of magazines—general, specialized, local, regional, or national—as well as newspapers, regularly publish articles related to money: earning it, managing it, or simply spending it. Whether you deal with something as simple as balancing your checkbook and paying household bills, or handle money on a business or professional level, there is a magazine that will be interested in a new angle in an article on financial matters. Many magazines are aimed at the consumer and discuss how money affects the lives of adults, couples, students, single parents, and even teenagers and younger children with allowances. Certainly, these magazines offer wide-ranging opportunities to the free-lance writer. Some personal experience articles require no research, but rather can focus on everyday financial problems: shopping, using coupons or not, supermarkets versus the neighborhood store for the least expensive marketing, almost any subject that will simplify or clarify the handling of money for the average person.

It will enlarge your prospect list in writing certain kinds of more complicated articles if you train yourself to be a good reporter with good research and interviewing skills. And an engaging, easy, readable style will work to your advantage in presenting ways that your readers will be helped in solving financial problems.

There are business magazines geared to such topics as investments, mortgages, and stocks and bonds, that require expertise so that any suggestions or recommendations you make (not on what stocks to buy, for example, but how to evaluate and balance your savings to bring you the greatest returns) will be authoritative. Careful research, interviews with bankers, brokers, people who run small businesses, and professionals who have to prepare departmental budgets in their work will help you gather enough facts and background material to write for even the more sophisticated reader.

Profiles, round-ups, service (how-to, where-to) pieces, personal experience articles, and features on money and the consumer all appear in different publications. In general, topics for money and consumer articles fall into two main categories: earning money and managing/spending it. To come up with ideas for money and consumer articles, observe your own life and the many ways it is affected by money. If you ran a successful yard sale, offer readers tips on how to go about it, how the pricing was done, whether you had any help or special problems with the buyers, and how you decided what would be the most profitable way of handling it. Did you combine your items with those of neighbors or friends and run a joint sale? Was it necessary to get some security?

When you were house-hunting, did you develop a system or worksheet and checklist that helped you decide the good points and weaknesses of the house and whether or not the price would match your budget? How did you get information about mortgage rates or get a knowledgeable person to check the condition of the house before you made an offer? Where did you go to get information about recent sales in the neighborhood and the prices that were paid? These are the kinds of questions that others in your situation would ask, and if you can supply the answers based on your experience, you can write a valuable article for any number of magazines.

What about the family clothes budget: How can you stretch it, and what suggestions can you make to a single parent or a couple with a limited income for stretching expendable income? Do you have a barter and swap system for clothes or toys in your P.T.A. or church? Practical answers to these questions are sought eagerly by readers, and therefore by many publications.

Other article possibilities include:

Earning money: How to start a home mail-order business; how to find a good part-time job that fits your regular commitments and responsibilities; a profile of a local restaurateur who, with the help of her staff and some local volunteers, rebuilt the restaurant after it had burned to the ground; a profile of the first woman stockbroker in your town; a round-up built around answers from recent college graduates on what their dream job might be; a how-to piece telling college or high school graduates how to prepare for and conduct themselves in a job interview to increase their chances of getting the job; a profile of high school students who have started their own business; a feature on how having an unemployed parent affects the rest of the family (not only their income but their relationships); a round-up that asks employers at large and small companies whether they believe they should offer on-site day care for employees' children; how to work successfully at a job or profession and still allow time for hobbies, outside interests, and spending time with the family; a round-up on the kind of volunteer service various neighbors or colleagues perform for the community; a personal experience piece on how you started your own, now successful candlemaking (or other) business with only a $100.00 investment; a profile or feature on the "garage" or "attic" hobby that becomes a commercial success, such as Blanchard's dressings, Sara Lee baked goods, or Ben & Jerry's ice cream.

Managing/spending money: how to choose the best savings/investment plan to prepare for a child's college education; how to manage a budget on a fixed income; how to stretch limited income with sound short-term investments; a survey of the best credit cards (those with low rates, no membership fee, etc.); how to use a credit card properly; a profile of an obsessive coupon clipper (including how much money he or she saves by using coupons); how to choose the best value in health (or home, life, auto) insurance; a feature on the economic plight of the elderly in today's society, but from a new, specific angle, like managing the costs incurred by a caretaker; a related topic on the problem of a chronically ill member of the household—a child, aunt, grandparent, parent, or even a close friend or companion; how to go about collecting overdue child support or alimony payments; how to make ends meet as a single parent; how to balance your children's needs with your own, especially if you are a working mother who has to dress well and arrange for child care; how this affects your marketing and meal preparation, where you shop, etc.; how to respond to children's demands for name-brand clothes or toys that their friends have or that they see advertised on television; teaching children how to manage their own money (how much allowance should they receive at various ages). When and what do they have to pay for from their own earnings and savings? At what age should they have their own checking and savings accounts? How do you choose the best values of any number of products and still stay within a budget? (This could include cars, television sets, bicycles, car seats, power tools, to name only a few.) What about house repairs: How long can you let them go and how can you get fairly priced but good quality work done?

This covers only a small portion of the possible topics you can write about and for which there is an eager audience—and a large one that changes constantly. This means that editors need to offer the same topics from time to time (but not too frequently and from a new angle).

As you think about writing articles on money matters, keep the following suggestions in mind:

1. Read local, regional, and some large-circulation city newspapers to keep up with the business and economic trends in your area as well as nationally. Reading advertisements as well as editorial material will give you clues to new products, as well as financial problems affecting large groups of people (unemployment, health care, etc.).

2. Keep up with friends, relatives or colleagues in vari-

ous occupations and professions; they may be able to provide you with information you need for your money or consumer articles. If you once worked full time in a field, stay in touch with former co-workers, customers, clients, even competitors, but make a point of developing new contacts as well. A free-lancer who specializes in this field writes, "A lot depends on bits and pieces of information you pick up by the grapevine."

3. Articles about money should not just be facts and numbers and statistics; ultimately they must show how these "facts" and trends impinge on people's lives. Relate statistics to people, and use anecdotes about them whenever possible. For example, if you are writing about savings or insurance plans or financing a new house or special programs to help accumulate enough money at the right time to pay for college education, include an anecdote or human interest story about families who have actually used such plans successfully.

4. Make your writing style lively and engaging, so the facts and statistics will be easily "digested" and understood.

5. If your article would be enhanced by using a chart or a graph showing prices or trends over a period of time, suggest this to the editor; provide a rough sketch with this type of information set forth so it can be created in final form by the staff of the magazine or newspaper.

Markets

To sum up: There are a vast number of markets for articles on money matters and finance; these range from general magazines and small newspapers to the regional and specialized publications and newsletters and major magazines of a national type. The subject pervades every social and economic level. Magazines like *Better Homes and Gardens,* as well as *Kiplinger's Personal Finance* and *Consumers Digest* publish articles on money, personal finance, mortgages, money management, and consumer issues related to money matters. Regional magazines like *Down East* and women's magazines like *Working Mother, Cosmopolitan,* and *Self* also publish these articles. Obviously, you should read thoroughly any of the magazines or newspapers that you plan to query with your article idea.

Hundreds of specialized publications, trade journals and professional magazines publish articles dealing with a particular business, field or industry. To write for these trade magazines, you should have some background, preferably work experience, in the field (computers, retailing, insurance, banking, to name only a few), or have access to experienced people and experts in a given business whom you can interview. Trade magazines are listed in such directories as the *Business Periodical Index* (Wilson Co., publishers), *Gale Directory of Publications and Broadcast Media,* and *Gebbie Press All-In-One Directory,* found in many large public library or college reference departments. The range of trade magazines is tremendous, including such titles as *Computer Currents* (there are several hundred publications in the computer field alone), *Banking Week, The American Salesman, Food Management, Barron's, Business Today, Dairy Foods Management, Greenhouse Management, Hardware Trade, Health Foods Business, Maintenance Technology, Independent Business, Modern Tire Dealer, Pizza Today, Pets/Supplies/Marketing, Roofer Magazine*—and more and more and more. Interestingly enough, although these sometimes require expert knowledge and know-how, articles often deal in a readable way with aspects that a writer interested in a field can learn about by studying back issues and doing related research or interviews with people who are experienced in these areas. Don't overlook special libraries (business branches of public libraries, corporate or industry libraries to which you may have access, like those in your own company or that you can get permission to use) for other resources.

18

SCIENCE AND NATURE

SCIENCE AND NATURE SURROUND US and affect our daily lives in various forms: weather, medicine, the environment, agriculture, etc. As a free-lance writer, you can learn how to write about science and nature, and you can sell your articles to a wide variety of publications, both technical and general.

Reading newspapers and magazines and observing the influence of science and nature on your own life are the best ways to find and develop your ideas for articles. For example, why did the storm that was predicted blow out to sea instead of striking your area? Why are weather predictions often wrong, especially in certain parts of the country? Have you had asbestos or lead paint removed from your home? What about the radon scare—is it justified? Have you had your house checked for it? Is there a landfill in your town? Should you have your lawn chemically treated for weeds? Have you or a relative or friend been given a new or still experimental treatment for a medical condition? What happened? Do lightning rods prevent houses from being damaged by lightning? How do smoke alarms work? Do you have a problem with raccoons on your property? If so, what have you done about it? Consider a profile of a local weather forecaster (How did he or she get to be a forecaster?) or the manager of a nuclear power plant, or a radiologist who has used new diagnostic technology—how has this technology improved medical treatment? Is there any explanation for the increase in earthquakes and tornadoes? How about a news story on the delayed launching of a weather station—who is affected by it? An article on how to shop for energy-efficient appliances and whether they are useful in environmental terms? Or how about a feature on "red tide" that each year damages shellfish and thus the fishing industry? The return of the gypsy moth? The spread of equine encephalitis? Lyme disease? All of these—and hundreds more—are possible topics for science and nature articles. Put your observations and imagination to work!

Above all, be sure to relate your topic to its effect on people. Science writing for all but highly technical, scientific publications is really about people and the natural world. So, if you write an article on how computers are being used in elementary schools, tell how and why, and be sure to include comments by teachers who like or dislike the computers and children who are being trained from age six for the computer world. Is it too soon? Who trains the teachers?

Sometimes a good science article for the lay reader (not the trained scientist) hardly seems like a science article. It cuts through jargon, uses analogies and anecdotes to help readers understand complex concepts, and explains in clear, straightforward language. Of course, reducing a complicated idea (like a new genetic discovery or a cure for AIDS) to its essence takes skill and background knowledge, but you can acquire these with lots of practice, good planning, and diligence. Here are a few suggestions to keep in mind:

1. Research your subject at the library, and write to nonprofit organizations, utility companies, research hospitals, the Centers for Disease Control, government agencies, or other sources that can supply you with information for your topic. Read the science section of good newspapers like *The New York Times*. If your article deals with conserving energy, write to your local gas, electric, or telephone company for information that relates to the subject. Even the leaflets that come with your bill often discuss these subjects. Do detailed research before you interview a scientist or other expert so you can ask intelligent questions to fill in the gaps in your library research. And don't be afraid to ask as many questions as you need in order to understand a concept, discovery, invention, or process. You won't be able to describe it clearly to readers if you don't understand it yourself.

2. Clearly define any scientific terms you must use, and try not to use too many in one sentence. Substitute common terms when possible. The editor of a prominent conservation journal says that a good article "goes into science somewhat but stays within layman's terms."

3. Present just one scientific or abstract concept at a time and whenever possible, link it to a concrete analogy, example, or anecdote. For example, to illustrate the amount of garbage that is generated by humans, you can tell readers that the entire commercial U.S. airline fleet could be rebuilt every three months just by using discarded aluminum cans.

4. Use the active voice in writing your article. This can be a problem in science writing, because scientists often

couch their statements in passive voice in an effort to be as accurate and precise as possible. Although they might know that a scientific or natural event occurs, they might not know how or why or cannot identify the agent that caused it to happen, so they cannot make the statement in active voice. When interviewing a scientist, try to get him or her to be as specific as possible, as long as the information is accurate.

5. Be careful to maintain your objectivity when writing about a scientific controversy or recent discovery. Be sure to present a balance of opinions and ideas, and distinguish clearly between theory and fact.

6. If a graph or chart would enhance the effectiveness of your article, provide sketches. If a sidebar would add to the article, include one that could be incorporated into the article if the editor chooses to do so.

All kinds of magazines and newspapers publish articles about science and nature. Your local newspaper, general magazines, women's magazines, health magazines, and regional magazines all offer a variety of these articles to their readers, as well as information about new discoveries, patents, or inventions. In addition, more specialized magazines such as *Omni, Environment,* and *Technology Review* publish articles on a variety of scientific topics. Of course, read the publications before querying so that you know the audience and requirements of each.

Selling Your Article

19

FINDING MARKETS

As a writer, you should have as your objective communicating with readers: to make a point, to provide facts, to explain how or where to do something, or to inform readers about an issue, event, or situation. To do this, you need to find the right market—that is, the most suitable publication (or publications) for your article idea; your audience is the publication's readers. As you develop your idea and write your article, you should always keep your market and audience in mind.

This book has stressed the most important rule in considering markets for article ideas: Study each magazine or newspaper carefully before querying the editor. Read several issues, including the articles, letters to the editor, editorial page, and even the advertisements. Write for a sample copy if the magazine is not on the newsstand or in the library; and write for guidelines once you have studied the publication itself.

The specialty chapters in Part Three of this book introduced you to specific markets for those fields. This chapter describes in more detail the general categories of markets, or types of publications that are available to you as a free-lance writer. In addition, consult *The Writer's Handbook,* published by The Writer, Inc., for hundreds of specific markets for your articles, or *The Writer* Magazine, which publishes monthly lists of free-lance markets in various fields.

GENERAL-INTEREST PUBLICATIONS

General-interest publications are aimed at a mass audience and cover topics in a variety of areas, from current events to lifestyles. They also publish articles in specialty areas, such as health care and science, that are of interest to the general public.

Even general-interest publications have a clear focus aimed at a particular (though wide) audience. For example, *US* magazine concentrates on articles about celebrities and entertainment; *Ebony* magazine publishes articles on African-American issues; *American Heritage* looks for articles on the history of American life and culture; *The Atlantic* uses in-depth pieces on public issues; and magazines like *Family Circle* publish general-interest articles with an emphasis on family and home life. When developing ideas for general-interest publications, it's vital to remember the focus and audience.

These publications are the most widely read and pay the highest rates for articles. They are also highly competitive and usually publish articles by established writers, but they are goals that any free-lance writer can aspire to.

WOMEN'S AND MEN'S MAGAZINES

Women's and men's magazines buy articles on all sorts of subjects, from fitness to personal finance, but these articles must be directly related to a male or female audience. For example, *Good Housekeeping* publishes articles for women who are interested or involved in marriage and family relationships; *Working Woman* is aimed at young professional women, while *Ms.* is concerned with issues of feminism and the changing social roles of women. Consider also the age of the audience. *Self* is designed for young women and focuses on health, nutrition, and fitness, while *Lear's* covers many of the same topics for older women.

The variety in tone and focus is just as great among the men's magazines. Some have a fashion and lifestyle focus, others emphasize sports, business, adventure, or erotica.

NEWSPAPERS

Newspapers provide a terrific opportunity for aspiring free-lance article writers. Although a newspaper generally has a staff of reporters who write articles, staff reporters can't cover all the stories that need to be told. Thus, the newspaper editor often depends on free-lance writers to fill in the gaps in such areas as travel, home decorating, pets, gardening, health, money, and personal problems. A weekly newspaper is an especially good place for free-lance writers to begin gathering publishing credits.

Because newspapers depend on timeliness even more than magazines do, writing for a newspaper usually means that you must research a topic and write your piece fairly quickly—sometimes in a week or less—and your article is published soon thereafter. Feature articles that are not timely, however, may be submitted any time after querying and getting a go-ahead.

Take a look at several newspapers from your region. Note that they publish articles on a wide range of topics, including current events, sports, health, science, travel, home and garden. Larger newspapers usually have an editor for each department; smaller newspapers may have only one or two editors for the entire paper. Thus, in aiming for the larger papers, you might work with more that one editor if you write articles in different fields—travel, health, home and garden, science, for instance.

Newspapers generally pay writers much less than magazines do, but newspaper articles are often shorter than magazine articles, so if you are a beginning writer, the opportunity to establish yourself will most likely outweigh the consideration of pay rates.

REGIONAL AND LOCAL PUBLICATIONS

Regional publications serve a particular geographic area. Local politics, environmental concerns, city building plans—virtually any issue of interest to a community could interest the editor of a regional publication. Regionals may be distributed just to readers in that area or they may reach readers throughout the country. *Yankee Magazine*, for example, focuses on topics related to New England, but its subscribers are located all over the United States. There are usually several magazines devoted to a specific region, so it's important to know the distinguishing focus of each. *Garden State Home & Garden* publishes pieces that center on decorating, design, and gardening in New Jersey; *New Jersey Good Life* focuses more on entertainment and dining; *New Jersey Reporter* publishes in-depth articles on the state's politics and public affairs; and *New Jersey Monthly* emphasizes general-interest articles, profiles, and service pieces for local readers. The tone and editorial concerns of each of the four magazines are distinct, though the readership may overlap.

The names of some magazines will tell you exactly

what region and editorial slant they represent; for example, it's hard to mistake the emphasis of *North Texas Golfer, Dallas Life Magazine, Florida Home and Garden*. On the other hand, you have to read sample copies of *San Diego Reader* or *Texas Monthly* to know if the emphasis is more on local business or local personalities. And you'd have to know something about the vernacular of Maine to recognize the title of *Down East*.

Read several issues of a local or regional publication to get the feel and flavor of the area, its special interests, "folkways," and attitudes before querying. Local publications obviously serve a smaller geographic area than do regional publications. They're a great place for a new writer to get started in article writing. Don't overlook your local weekly or daily newspaper; it may not pay a lot (or at all, at the outset), but many writers establish themselves by writing first for their town papers, often with a book review or short feature or profile of an unusual local citizen. Issues that become political offer good ways to start with a round-up piece.

Inflight Magazines

Inflight magazines are available free to airline passengers. It's obvious that these magazines publish travel pieces, but they also publish articles on a wide variety of subjects, including business, home, science, health, arts, and sports, especially in the major cities or areas served by a specific airline. These articles are usually shorter than regular features in other magazines, and generally do not deal with controversial subjects (they are meant to entertain and inform the traveler with lighter reading). Inflight magazines include *USAIR, Aboard, American Way,* and *Sky*. A request to the airline will bring you sample copies. Almost every major airline and many smaller ones publish magazines. It's worth sending letters and self-addressed, stamped postcards to a few airlines to find out if they have magazines.

BUSINESS AND TRADE PUBLICATIONS

There are virtually hundreds of trade journals—covering every trade, from banking to farming to manufacturing to construction—and they offer free-lance writers a vast and diverse market. Trade journals tend to be focused and well defined—*American Farriers Journal, Campground Management, Art Business News, Real Estate Today*—and the editors are on the lookout for specific, relevant articles.

Business magazines are more general in focus. *Business Today, Business Times, Barron's,* and *Across the Board* publish articles on financial news from a national angle. Writers who can turn financial advice and technical business how-to into clear prose are in high demand at both trade publications and business magazines.

Gebbie Press All-In-One Directory, which can be found in large public libraries' reference departments, lists trade and business publications around the country. The competition at national business magazines can be fierce; however, regional business magazines and specialized trade journals are much more receptive to free-lance work. Obtain and study the publications in fields you want to write for. They may offer you the opportunity to write about a subject that you are already somewhat familiar with.

COLLEGE, LITERARY, AND LITTLE MAGAZINES

Literary journals, including college and "little" magazines, also buy material from free-lance writers. *The International Directory of Little Magazines and Small*

Presses, published annually by Dustbooks (usually found in library reference rooms), contains nearly 1,000 pages of listings for these publications, which welcome material from beginning writers as well as professionals. Payment is usually low, often in copies of the issue in which published work appears, but publication in a literary journal can lead to recognition by the editors of larger magazines, who read the little magazines in their search for new talent.

Religious Magazines

Editors of religious and denominational publications rely heavily on free-lance material, on subjects ranging from biblical interpretation to general-interest articles. Inspirational pieces that encourage the reader to apply religious principles to daily life; personal experience pieces with an inspirational slant; educational articles; and discussions of social concerns are all topics that religious publications address. Some of these magazines are community- or family-oriented; others are for or about specific faiths. As always, it is important to be familiar with a publication before querying the editor.

Specialty Publications

A growing number of publications cater to special interests, and a growing number of writers are developing their own specialties. There are publications specializing in a vast range of subjects, including those dealt with in detail in this book: travel and recreation, sports and fitness, health, hobbies, crafts and collectibles, home and garden, money and the consumer, and science and nature. Other specialties include automotive, animals, the arts, and history. In fact, the list seems nearly endless. Within a broad area, there are publications that focus on more narrow aspects of a specialty. It's important to study the publications of your specialty thoroughly in order to get to know the market and audience for each.

As you can see, the opportunities for you to sell your free-lance articles are legion. So do your homework: Spend time in the periodical room of any library you have access to; browse through magazines at newsstands, then buy a few that interest you and study both the articles and the advertisements. Send for writing guidelines and then query an editor with your idea. Above all, keep trying, and be optimistic. There is bound to be a market out there for your article.

20

THE BUSINESS SIDE—
DOLLARS AND SENSE

WRITING FOR PUBLICATION HAS A BUSINESS SIDE, and as a professional you need to know some of the basics. When an editor gives you the go-ahead to write an article, it's appropriate to ask how much payment you can expect for an accepted piece. (You may already have an idea of the publication's pay range from writers' guidelines if you have requested them in advance.) Magazines and newspapers often have different rates of pay for different types of articles; for example, they'll usually pay more for a full-length feature than for a short personal experience piece. Some publications pay more to established writers or to those who have written for them previously. When you discuss money with the editor, don't be shy. This is a business arrangement. Ask what the usual range of payment is and where your article, if accepted, might fit on the scale. Although in some cases you might suggest a higher fee than offered, don't *demand* it, unless you are prepared to have the editor turn you down and possibly be reluctant to consider you for future projects.

Instead of thinking only about the dollar amount an editor has offered you, look at the value of your article in a variety of ways. You might accept a lower fee from a prestigious magazine or newspaper in order to get your foot in the door at that publication and add to your writing credits. Or you might accept a smaller fee for a piece on a subject that you know thoroughly and can, therefore, write about in a short period of time. If you're an expert cyclist and an editor has asked you to write a short piece on how to change a bicycle tire (which you've done yourself dozens of times), you could probably write the article in an hour, and the lower rate might be perfectly acceptable.

Don't assume that the publication will pay your expenses for phone calls, postage, or travel involved in writing your article. If you anticipate incurring these expenses, ask the editor about them in advance. Expenses are rarely, if ever, paid to new or unestablished writers, but if the publication does agree to reimburse you for expenses, keep meticulous records and receipts. Don't take advantage of an expense account; it isn't a blank check.

Make sure you are clear about the publication's payment policy—on acceptance or on publication. Ideally, you should be paid on acceptance, but many publications don't work this way. "Acceptance" may mean "after rewrites." Or you may be paid upon publication, when your piece actually appears in print. Obviously, payment on publication is less desirable, since you could wait up to a year for a check if your article is published that long after it is accepted. Most magazines and newspapers have set policies about this, and there isn't much you can do to change them; but it helps to know ahead. And if you don't receive your check on time, keep phoning and writing until you do. Make a pleasant pest of yourself until you have that check in hand.

Contracts: Written or Verbal?

All agreements, verbal and written, are based on trust. The editor expects you to write the article you've agreed to and deliver it on time. You trust the editor to publish your article and pay you the agreed-upon amount at the appropriate time.

But even the best intentions of writer and editor sometimes break down: The editor could move to another department or leave the publication altogether; or the publication might change some of its policies while you're working on your article. Thus, even if the magazine or newspaper doesn't use written contracts, it's always a good practice to follow up any verbal agreement with a letter to the editor, outlining the terms as you understand them. That way, both parties are clear about the points of agreement, even if circumstances change partway through your work on the article.

It the editor sends you a written contract, *read it carefully.* Don't let your excitement over your success cloud your judgment. Make sure that the contract states the terms that you and the editor had previously agreed to. If the contract includes provisions or terms that you had not previously discussed or don't understand or agree with, call or write the editor to get the matter clarified.

Rights

Publication rights are the legal rights that a magazine or newspaper has to your article. Normally, a magazine or newspaper buys the right to publish your article once; this is referred to as "first North American serial rights." After that, all other rights in the article are yours. Occasionally, the standard, written contract you receive from a publication asks for additional rights: electronic, republication, foreign language rights, reprints in various forms and some not specifically stated. Check this with the editor. If the publication wants to use your article more than once, it must pay an additional amount over the basic fee. Otherwise, you can ask the editor to delete such phrases from the contract.

Making a Living

How much money can you make from your article writing? Some new writers have exaggerated—and unrealistic—ideas about what they can or will earn from the articles they sell. Others feel so grateful to have their work accepted that they fail to read the contracts or agreements carefully *before* signing them, and they lose out on money they legitimately deserve. The amount of money you can make depends on the pay scales of the publications you write for, the demand for articles on your subject, your ability and success in selling what you write, your experience as a writer, and your skill in negotiating agreements. Your earnings will fall somewhere between wealth and poverty: In short, until you are a published writer, there is no way to predict how much money you will make.

At the beginning, gaining credits from sales to any of

the thousands of magazines and newspapers available to free-lance writers is the primary goal. Most writers start out by writing just a few articles a year, augmenting their full-time jobs; many continue this pace throughout their careers and can make a steady income if they are diligent and seek out a variety of markets, some of which, though small, pay relatively well. Others make the jump to full-time writing sooner, if they sell regularly to higher-paying publications. Only you can decide which will work for you. Part of this decision, of course, depends upon how good a writer you are and on the income you require. Full-time free-lance writing isn't glamorous. It involves hard work and uncertain financial returns, but it provides flexibility and the satisfaction of making a living at what you love to do. "This is all a house of cards," says one full-time free-lance writer with many articles to his credit. "There's always that little rat gnawing at you. Maybe it keeps you honest. My fondest dream is that someday I'll have made enough money to write just what I want. Not chained to my desk trying to pump out so many words, always behind."

National Writers Union

The National Writers Union (13 Astor Place, 7th floor, New York, NY 10003) is a collective bargaining unit that strives to keep its members informed about the publishing business, helps them improve contract terms, and settles disputes between writers and publishers whenever possible. Some writers feel that being members provides them with support; others prefer to rely on their own skills and experience in dealing with the business side of writing.

Record-Keeping

As a selling free-lance writer, full- or part-time, you need to keep track of your income and expenses, as you must pay taxes quarterly, on estimated income.

Keep scrupulous records. Set up your own system for recording expenses and filing receipts, and stick to it. Don't wait until the night before your taxes are due to sift through a shoebox of receipts and notations on napkins. You'll save yourself many headaches by maintaining your records as you go.

Consult an accountant or the IRS with any questions you have about the tax implications of your earnings from article writing. The amounts and methods of payment will depend on whether you write part-time or full-time, as well as your income combined with your salary from a regular job.

21

COPING WITH FAILURE—AND SUCCESS

WRITING IS A SERIES OF UPS AND DOWNS. No writer gets everything published; yet most writers who are intelligent and persist in an orderly way do begin to sell their work. The important thing is to learn from both the failures and the successes.

Every writer has at least a small collection of rejection slips. Some are impersonal postcards, others are friendly, encouraging letters from editors. When you receive a rejection of a query or an unsolicited manuscript, let yourself be disappointed. It's only natural. But then pick yourself up and dust yourself off. See what you can learn from the rejection. Unfortunately, most editors do not have time to respond or comment on writers' material in detail. However, an editor may jot a comment to you that tells you why the material was rejected. If the editor says that your query or article wasn't appropriate for the magazine, go back to the magazine and study it again. It's quite likely you'll see where you missed the boat. At this point, see if your query or article, with some revising or refocusing, might be made appropriate for another magazine or newspaper. In some cases, revisions may even help you sell the piece to another *department* of the magazine that initially rejected it. If so, make the necessary changes and send it out.

Never waste anything you've written, rejected or otherwise. The experience has increased your knowledge and skill as a writer and a researcher. You may have learned more about a subject area even if it didn't bring you a byline and a check. And you might use the research or some of the written material in another piece.

Writing is a lonely job. Sometimes it's tough to keep going in the face of uncertainty and obscurity, but determination has a way of paying off. If you want to be a writer, you must write. No one else can accomplish it for you. You have to sit down and do it.

You publish your first article, and you wait for the phone calls from family, friends, and colleagues praising you as the best new writer of the decade. But the phone is silent. The world goes on, oblivious to your brilliant prose. A few days pass, and when you meet a close friend, you wait politely, giving the person every opportunity to mention your published piece; but the person says nothing about it. You're deflated. How could he or she be so insensitive?

Or you do get several phone calls and a few letters. But they aren't filled with unqualified praise. A friend disagrees with your stance on an environmental issue. Your sister misses the point of your article and seems offended by it. A colleague sniffs and says, "I could have written a better article than that." If this is success, you wonder, why write again?

Just as coping with rejection requires a slightly tough

skin, so does coping with success. As a published writer, you're going to get all kinds of responses to your writing, from indifferent to impassioned. Do your best to put these in perspective. An experienced writer I know simply doesn't reply to angry letters, but tries to understand the context in which people write these. "All readings are autobiographical," he observes. "There isn't one, single truth in life. People all read their own truths." Readers bring to each piece of writing a whole set of biases, past experiences, and opinions, both conscious and unconscious. Thus, nothing is read in a vacuum, and each reading is unique.

When I complained about indifference to or jealousy over my first book, a friend advised, "Get new friends." She had a point. I didn't drop my old friends, but I subsequently didn't expect so much of them. And I found a few new friends who understood the time and effort it had taken to write a book and who had the insight to comment on it. But I also made a strict rule for myself: Never ask people what they think of what I've written. Harsh experience caused me to establish this rule, and sticking to it has proved to be a good practice.

Constructive criticism, even if it's painful, is often instructive. Good criticism can help you become a better writer. So pay attention to readers whose opinions you value. Be honest with yourself. If someone points out a way that you can improve your writing technique next time around, accept it—gracefully.

Praise does come to the published writer, sometimes from the most unlikely places. My auto mechanic told me that he reads all my newspaper columns and loves them. An eleven-year-old girl announced to me that she planned to do a book report on my first book. Not everyone is comfortable with praise, but a kind word from either a loved one or a stranger makes up for the daggers of unconstructive criticism. You do write to be read; and when you know you have entertained, touched, or taught a reader something new, that's success.

And when you've faced that blank page and stared it down, forced the words onto it and said what you wanted to say, you can put down your pen, click off the typewriter or computer, shut off the light. You'll tackle the whole process again tomorrow because you've discovered the joy of writing. You're a professional writer.